THE MAN ARCHAN

AND OTHER TALES OF ADVENTURE

SIR ARTHUR CONAN DOYLE

[ZHINGOORA BOOKS]

The digital and paperback edition is published by Zhingoora Books

The Cover is Designed by Pallav Sethiya.

zhingoora_books@yahoo.com

CONTENTS

By SIR ARTHUR CONAN DOYLE

I

THE DÉBUT OF BIMBASHI JOYCE

It was in the days when the tide of Mahdism, which had swept in such a flood from the great Lakes and Darfur to the confines of Egypt, had at last come to its full, and even begun, as some hoped, to show signs of a turn. At its outset it had been terrible. It had engulfed Hicks's army, swept over Gordon and Khartoum, rolled behind the British forces as they retired down the river, and finally cast up a spray of raiding parties as far north as Assouan. Then it found other channels to east and to west, to Central Africa and to Abyssinia, and retired a little on the side of Egypt. For ten years there ensued a lull, during which the frontier garrisons looked out upon those distant blue hills of Dongola. Behind the violet mists which draped them, lay a land of blood and horror. From time to time some adventurer went south towards those haze-girt mountains, tempted by stories of gum and ivory, but none ever returned. Once a mutilated Egyptian and once a Greek woman, mad with thirst and fear, made their way to the lines. They were the only exports of that country of darkness. Sometimes the sunset would turn those distant mists into a bank of crimson, and the dark mountains would rise from that sinister reek like islands in a sea of blood. It seemed a grim symbol in the southern heaven when seen from the fort-capped hills by Wady Halfa.

Ten years of lust in Khartoum, ten years of silent work in Cairo, and then all was ready, and it was time for civilisation to take a trip south once more, travelling, as her wont is, in an armoured train. Everything was ready, down to the last pack-saddle of the last camel, and yet no one suspected it, for an unconstitutional Government has its advantages. A great administrator had argued, and managed, and cajoled; a great soldier had organised and planned, and made piastres do the work of pounds. And then one night these two master spirits met and clasped hands, and the soldier vanished away upon some business of his own. And just at that very time Bimbashi Hilary Joyce, seconded from the Royal Mallow Fusiliers, and temporarily attached to the Ninth Soudanese, made his first appearance in Cairo.

Napoleon had said, and Hilary Joyce had noted, that great reputations are only to be made in the East. Here he was in the East with four tin cases of baggage, a Wilkinson sword, a Bond's slug-throwing pistol, and a copy of Green's Introduction to the Study of Arabic. With such a start, and the blood of youth running hot in his veins, everything seemed easy. He was a little frightened of the General, he had heard stories of his sternness to young officers, but with tact and suavity he hoped for the best. So, leaving his effects at Shepheard's Hotel, he reported himself at headquarters.

It was not the General, but the head of the Intelligence Department who received him, the Chief being still absent upon that business which had called him. Hilary Joyce found himself in the presence of a short, thick-set officer, with a gentle voice and a placid expression which covered a remarkably acute and energetic spirit. With that quiet smile and guileless manner he had undercut and outwitted the most cunning of Orientals. He stood, a cigarette between his fingers, looking at the new-comer.

"I heard that you had come. Sorry the Chief isn't here to see you. Gone up to the frontier, you know."

"My regiment is at Wady Halfa. I suppose, sir, that I should report myself there at once?"

"No; I was to give you your orders." He led the way to a map upon the wall, and pointed with the end of his cigarette. "You see this place. It's the Oasis of Kurkur—a little quiet, I am afraid, but excellent air. You are to get out there as quick as possible. You'll find a company of the Ninth, and half a squadron of cavalry. You will be in command."

Hilary Joyce looked at the name, printed at the intersection of two black lines, without another dot upon the map for several inches round it.

"A village, sir?"

"No, a well. Not very good water, I'm afraid, but you soon get accustomed to natron. It's an important post, as being at the junction of two caravan routes. All routes are closed now, of course, but still you never know who might come along them."

"We are there, I presume, to prevent raiding?"

"Well, between you and me, there's really nothing to raid. You are there to intercept messengers. They must call at the wells. Of course you have only just come out, but you probably understand already enough about the conditions of this country to know that there is a great deal of disaffection about, and that the Khalifa is likely to try and keep in touch with his adherents. Then, again, Senoussi lives up that way"—he waved his cigarette to the westward—"the Khalifa might send a message to him along that route. Anyhow, your duty is to arrest every one coming along, and get some account of him before you let him go. You don't talk Arabic, I suppose?"

"I am learning, sir."

"Well, well, you'll have time enough for study there. And you'll have a native officer, Ali something or other, who speaks English, and can interpret for you. Well, good-bye—I'll tell the Chief that you reported yourself. Get on to your post now as quickly as you can."

Railway to Baliani, the post-boat to Assouan, and then two days on a camel in the Libyan Desert, with an Ababdeh guide, and three baggage-camels to tie one down to their own exasperating pace. However, even two and a half miles an hour mount up in time, and at last, on the third evening, from the blackened slag-heap of a hill which is called the Jebel Kurkur, Hilary Joyce looked down upon a distant clump of palms, and thought that this cool patch of green in the midst of the merciless blacks and yellows was the fairest colour effect that he had ever seen. An hour later he had ridden into the little camp, the guard had turned out to salute him, his native subordinate had greeted him in excellent English, and he had fairly entered into his own.

It was not an exhilarating place for a lengthy residence. There was one large bowl shaped, grassy depression sloping down to the three pits of brown and brackish water. There was the grove of palm trees also, beautiful to look upon, but exasperating in view of the fact that Nature has provided her least shady trees on the very spot where shade is needed most. A single widespread acacia did something to restore the balance. Here Hilary Joyce slumbered in the heat, and in the cool he inspected his square-shouldered, spindle-shanked Soudanese, with their cheery black faces and their funny little pork-pie forage caps. Joyce was a martinet at drill, and the blacks loved being drilled, so the Bimbashi was soon popular among them. But one day was exactly like another. The weather, the view, the employment, the food—everything was the same. At the end of three weeks he felt that he had been there for interminable years. And then at last there came something to break the monotony.

One evening, as the sun was sinking, Hilary Joyce rode slowly down the old caravan road. It had a fascination for him, this narrow track, winding among the boulders and curving up the nullahs, for he remembered how in the map it had gone on and on, stretching away into the unknown heart of Africa. The countless pads of innumerable camels through many centuries had beaten it smooth, so that now, unused and deserted, it still wound away, the strangest of roads, a foot broad, and perhaps two thousand miles in length. Joyce wondered as he rode how long it was since any traveller had journeyed up it from the south, and then he raised his eyes, and there was a man coming along the path.

For an instant Joyce thought that it might be one of his own men, but a second glance assured him that this could not be so. The stranger was dressed in the flowing robes of an Arab, and not in the close-fitting khaki of a soldier. He was very tall, and a high turban made him seem gigantic. He strode swiftly along, with head erect, and the bearing of a man who knows no fear.

Who could he be, this formidable giant coming out of the unknown? The percursor possibly of a horde of savage spearmen. And where could he have walked from? The nearest well was a long hundred miles down the track. At any rate the frontier post of Kurkur could not afford to receive casual visitors. Hilary Joyce whisked round his horse, galloped into camp, and gave the alarm. Then, with twenty horsemen at his back, he rode out again to reconnoitre.

The man was still coming on in spite of these hostile preparations. For an instant he had hesitated when first he saw the cavalry, but escape was out of the question, and he advanced with the air of one who makes the best of a bad job. He made no resistance, and said nothing when the hands of two troopers clutched at his shoulders, but walked quietly between their horses into camp. Shortly afterwards the patrols came in again. There were no signs of any Dervishes. The man was alone. A splendid trotting camel had been found lying dead a little way down the track. The mystery of the stranger's arrival was explained. But why, and whence, and whither?—these were questions for which a zealous officer must find an answer.

Hilary Joyce was disappointed that there were no Dervishes. It would have been a great start for him in the Egyptian army had he fought a little action on his own account. But even as it was, he had a rare chance of impressing the authorities. He would love to show his capacity to the head of the Intelligence, and even more to that grim Chief who never forgot what was smart, or forgave what was slack. The prisoner's dress and bearing showed that he was of importance. Mean men do not ride pure-bred trotting camels. Joyce sponged his head with cold water, drank a cup of strong coffee, put on an imposing official tarboosh instead of his sun-helmet, and formed himself into a court of inquiry and judgment under the acacia tree.

He would have liked his people to have seen him now, with his two black orderlies in waiting, and his Egyptian native officer at his side. He sat behind a camp-table, and the prisoner, strongly guarded, was led up to him. The man was a handsome fellow, with bold grey eyes and a long black beard.

"Why!" cried Joyce, "the rascal is making faces at me."

A curious contraction had passed over the man's features, but so swiftly that it might have been a nervous twitch. He was now a model of Oriental gravity.

"Ask him who he is, and what he wants?"

The native officer did so, but the stranger made no reply, save that the same sharp spasm passed once more over his face.

"Well, I'm blessed!" cried Hilary Joyce. "Of all the impudent scoundrels! He keeps on winking at me. Who are you, you rascal? Give an account of yourself! D'ye hear?"

But the tall Arab was as impervious to English as to Arabic. The Egyptian tried again and again. The prisoner looked at Joyce with his inscrutable eyes, and occasionally twitched his face at him, but never opened his mouth. The Bimbashi scratched his head in bewilderment.

"Look here, Mahomet Ali, we've got to get some sense out of this fellow. You say there are no papers on him?"

"No, sir; we found no papers."

"No clue of any kind?"

"He has come far, sir. A trotting camel does not die easily. He has come from Dongola, at least."

"Well, we must get him to talk,"

"It is possible that he is deaf and dumb."

"Not he. I never saw a man look more all there in my life."

"You might send him across to Assouan."

"And give some one else the credit! No, thank you. This is my bird. But how are we going to get him to find his tongue?"

The Egyptian's dark eyes skirted the encampment and rested on the cook's fire.

"Perhaps," said he, "if the Bimbashi thought fit——" He looked at the prisoner and then at the burning wood.

"No, no, it wouldn't do. No, by Jove, that's going too far."

"A very little might do it."

"No, no. It's all very well here, but it would sound just awful if ever it got as far as Fleet Street. But, I say," he whispered, "we might frighten him a bit. There's no harm in that."

"No, sir."

"Tell them to undo the man's galabeeah. Order them to put a horseshoe in the fire and make it red-hot."

The prisoner watched the proceedings with an air which had more of amusement than of uneasiness. He never winced as the black sergeant approached with the glowing shoe held upon two bayonets.

"Will you speak now?" asked the Bimbashi savagely.

The prisoner smiled gently and stroked his beard.

"Oh, chuck the infernal thing away!" cried Joyce, jumping up in a passion. "There's no use trying to bluff the fellow. He knows we won't do it. But I can and I will flog him, and you tell him from me that if he hasn't found his tongue by to-morrow morning, I'll take the skin off his back as sure as my name's Joyce. Have you said all that?"

"Yes, sir."

"Well, you can sleep upon it, you beauty, and a good night's rest may it give you!"

He adjourned the Court, and the prisoner, as imperturbable as ever, was led away by the guard to his supper of rice and water.

Hilary Joyce was a kind-hearted man, and his own sleep was considerably disturbed by the prospect of the punishment which he must inflict next day. He had hopes that the mere sight of the koorbash and the thongs might prevail over his prisoner's obstinacy. And then, again, he thought how shocking it would be if the man proved to be really dumb after all. The possibility shook him so that he had almost determined by daybreak that he would send the stranger on unhurt to Assouan. And yet what a tame conclusion it would be to the incident! He lay upon his angareeb still debating it when the question suddenly and effectively settled itself. Ali Mahomet rushed into his tent.

"Sir," he cried, "the prisoner is gone!"

"Gone!"

"Yes, sir, and your own best riding camel as well. There is a slit cut in the tent, and he got away unseen in the early morning."

The Bimbashi acted with all energy. Cavalry rode along every track; scouts examined the soft sand of the wadys for signs of the fugitive, but no trace was discovered. The man had utterly disappeared. With a heavy heart Hilary Joyce wrote an official report of the matter and forwarded it to Assouan. Five days later there came a curt order from the Chief that he should report himself there. He feared the worst from the stern soldier, who spared others as little as he spared himself.

And his worst forebodings were realised. Travel-stained and weary, he reported himself one night at the General's quarters. Behind a table piled with papers and strewn with maps the famous soldier and his Chief of Intelligence were deep in plans and figures. Their greeting was a cold one.

"I understand, Captain Joyce," said the General, "that you have allowed a very important prisoner to slip through your fingers."

"I am sorry, sir."

"No doubt. But that will not mend matters. Did you ascertain anything about him before you lost him?"

"No, sir."

"How was that?"

"I could get nothing out of him, sir."

"Did you try?"

"Yes, sir; I did what I could."

"What did you do?"

"Well, sir, I threatened to use physical force."

"What did he say?"

"He said nothing."

"What was he like?"

"A tall man, sir. Rather a desperate character, I should think."

"Any way by which we could identify him?"

"A long black beard, sir. Grey eyes. And a nervous way of twitching his face."

"Well, Captain Joyce," said the General, in his stern, inflexible voice, "I cannot congratulate you upon your first exploit in the Egyptian army. You are aware that every English officer in this force is a picked man. I have the whole British army from which to draw. It is necessary, therefore, that I should insist upon the very highest efficiency. It would be unfair upon the others to pass over any obvious want of zeal or intelligence. You are seconded from the Royal Mallows, I understand?"

"Yes, sir."

"I have no doubt that your Colonel will be glad to see you fulfilling your regimental duties again."

Hilary Joyce's heart was too heavy for words. He was silent.

"I will let you know my final decision to-morrow morning."

Joyce saluted and turned upon his heel.

"You can sleep upon that, you beauty, and a good night's rest may it give you!"

Joyce turned in bewilderment. Where had those words been used before? Who was it who had used them?

The General was standing erect. Both he and the Chief of the Intelligence were laughing. Joyce stared at the tall figure, the erect bearing, the inscrutable grey eyes.

"Good Lord!" he gasped.

"Well, well, Captain Joyce, we are quits!" said the General, holding out his hand. "You gave me a bad ten minutes with that infernal red-hot horseshoe of yours. I've done as much for you. I don't think we can spare you for the Royal Mallows just yet awhile."

"But, sir; but——!"

"The fewer questions the better, perhaps. But of course it must seem rather amazing. I had a little private business with the Kabbabish. It must be done in person. I did it, and came to your post in my return. I kept on winking at you as a sign that I wanted a word with you alone."

"Yes, yes. I begin to understand."

"I couldn't give it away before all those blacks, or where should I have been the next time I used my false beard and Arab dress? You put me in a very awkward position. But at last I had a word alone with your Egyptian officer, who managed my escape all right."

"He! Mahomet Ali!"

"I ordered him to say nothing. I had a score to settle with you. But we dine at eight, Captain Joyce. We live plainly here, but I think I can do you a little better than you did me at Kurkur."

II

THE SURGEON OF GASTER FELL

I: HOW THE WOMAN CAME TO KIRKBY-MALHOUSE

Bleak and wind-swept is the little town of Kirkby-Malhouse, harsh and forbidding are the fells upon which it stands. It stretches in a single line of grey-stone, slate-roofed houses, dotted down the furze-clad slope of the rolling moor.

In this lonely and secluded village, I, James Upperton, found myself in the summer of '85. Little as the hamlet had to offer, it contained that for which I yearned above all things—seclusion and freedom from all which might distract my mind from the high and weighty subjects which engaged it. But the inquisitiveness of my landlady made my lodgings undesirable and I determined to seek new quarters.

As it chanced, I had in one of my rambles come upon an isolated dwelling in the very heart of these lonely moors, which I at once determined should be my own. It was a two-roomed cottage, which had once belonged to some shepherd, but had long been deserted, and was crumbling rapidly to ruin. In the winter floods, the Gaster Beck, which runs down Gaster Fell, where the little dwelling stood, had overswept its banks and torn away a part of the wall. The roof was in ill case, and the scattered slates lay thick amongst the grass. Yet the main shell of the house stood firm and true; and it was no great task for me to have all that was amiss set right.

The two rooms I laid out in a widely different manner—my own tastes are of a Spartan turn, and the outer chamber was so planned as to accord with them. An oil-stove by Rippingille of Birmingham furnished me with the means of cooking; while two great bags, the one of flour, and the other of potatoes, made me independent of all supplies from without. In diet I had long been a Pythagorean, so that the scraggy, long-limbed sheep which browsed upon the wiry grass by the Gaster Beck had little to fear from their new companion. A nine-gallon cask of oil served me as a sideboard; while a square table, a deal chair and a truckle-bed completed the list of my domestic fittings. At the head of my couch hung two unpainted shelves—the lower for my dishes and cooking utensils, the upper for the few portraits which took me back to the little that was pleasant in the long, wearisome toiling for wealth and for pleasure which had marked the life I had left behind.

If this dwelling-room of mine were plain even to squalor, its poverty was more than atoned for by the luxury of the chamber which was destined to serve me as my study. I had ever held that it was best for my mind to be surrounded by such objects as would be in harmony with the studies which occupied it, and that the loftiest and most ethereal conditions of thought are only possible amid surroundings which please the eye and gratify the senses. The room which I had set apart for my mystic studies was set forth in a style as gloomy and majestic as the thoughts and aspirations with which it was to harmonise. Both walls and ceilings were covered with a paper of the richest and glossiest black, on which was traced a lurid and arabesque pattern of dead gold. A black velvet curtain covered the single diamond-paned window; while a thick, yielding carpet of the same material prevented the sound of my own footfalls, as I paced backward and forward, from breaking the current of my thought. Along the cornices ran gold rods, from which depended six pictures, all of the sombre and imaginative caste, which chimed best with my fancy.

And yet it was destined that ere ever I reached this quiet harbour I should learn that I was still one of humankind, and that it is an ill thing to strive to break the bond which binds us to our fellows. It was but two nights before the date I had fixed upon for my change of dwelling, when I was conscious of a bustle in the house beneath, with the bearing of heavy burdens up the creaking stair, and the harsh voice of my landlady, loud in welcome and protestations of joy. From time to time, amid the whirl of words, I could hear a gentle and softly modulated voice, which struck pleasantly upon my ear after the long weeks during which I had listened only to the rude dialect of the dalesmen. For an hour I could hear the dialogue beneath—the high voice and the low, with clatter of cup and clink of spoon, until at last a light, quick step passed my study door, and I knew that my new fellow-lodger had sought her room.

On the morning after this incident I was up be-times, as is my wont; but I was surprised, on glancing from my window, to see that our new inmate was earlier still. She was walking down the narrow pathway, which zigzags over the fell—a tall woman, slender, her head sunk upon her breast, her arms filled with a bristle of wild flowers, which she had gathered in her morning rambles. The white and pink of her dress, and the touch of deep red ribbon in her broad drooping hat, formed a pleasant dash of colour against the dun-tinted landscape. She was some distance off when I first set eyes upon her, yet I knew that this wandering woman could be none other than our arrival of last night, for there was a grace and refinement in her bearing which marked her from the dwellers of the fells. Even as I watched she passed swiftly and lightly down the pathway, and turning through the wicket gate, at the further end of our cottage garden, she seated herself upon the green bank which faced my window, and strewing her flowers in front of her, set herself to arrange them.

As she sat there, with the rising sun at her back, and the glow of the morning spreading like an aureole around her stately and well-poised head, I could see that she was a woman of extraordinary personal beauty. Her face was Spanish rather than English in its type—oval, olive, with black, sparkling eyes, and a sweetly sensitive mouth. From under the broad straw hat two thick coils of blue-black hair curved down on either side of her graceful queenly neck. I was surprised, as I watched her, to see that her shoes and skirt bore witness to a journey rather than to a mere morning ramble. Her light dress was stained, wet and bedraggled; while her boots were thick with the yellow soil of the fells. Her face, too, wore a weary expression, and her young beauty seemed to be clouded over by the shadow of inward trouble. Even as I watched her, she burst suddenly into wild weeping, and throwing down her bundle of flowers ran swiftly into the house.

Distrait as I was and weary of the ways of the world, I was conscious of a sudden pang of sympathy and grief as I looked upon the spasm of despair which seemed to convulse this strange and beautiful woman. I bent to my books, and yet my thoughts would ever turn to her proud clear-cut face, her weather-stained dress, her drooping head, and the sorrow which lay in each line and feature of her pensive face.

Mrs. Adams, my landlady, was wont to carry up my frugal breakfast; yet it was very rarely that I allowed her to break the current of my thoughts, or to draw my mind by her idle chatter from weightier things. This morning, however, for once, she found me in a listening mood, and with little prompting, proceeded to pour into my ears all that she knew of our beautiful visitor.

"Miss Eva Cameron be her name, sir," she said: "but who she be, or where she came fra, I know little more than yoursel'. Maybe it was the same reason that brought her to Kirkby-Malhouse as fetched you there yoursel', sir."

"Possibly," said I, ignoring the covert question; "but I should hardly have thought that Kirkby-Malhouse was a place which offered any great attractions to a young lady."

"Heh, sir!" she cried, "there's the wonder of it. The leddy has just come fra France; and how her folk come to learn of me is just a wonder. A week ago, up comes a man to my door—a fine man, sir, and a gentleman, as one could see with half an eye. 'You are Mrs. Adams,' says he. 'I engage your rooms for Miss Cameron,' says he.

'She will be here in a week,' says he; and then off without a word of terms. Last night there comes the young leddy hersel'—soft-spoken and downcast, with a touch of the French in her speech. But my sakes, sir! I must away and mak' her some tea, for she'll feel lonesome-like, poor lamb, when she wakes under a strange roof."

II: HOW I WENT FORTH TO GASTER FELL

I was still engaged upon my breakfast when I heard the clatter of dishes and the landlady's footfall as she passed toward her new lodger's room. An instant afterward she had rushed down the passage and burst in upon me with uplifted hand and startled eyes. "Lord 'a mercy, sir!" she cried, "and asking your pardon for troubling you, but I'm feared o' the young leddy, sir; she is not in her room."

"Why, there she is," said I, standing up and glancing through the casement. "She has gone back for the flowers she left upon the bank."

"Oh, sir, see her boots and her dress!" cried the landlady wildly. "I wish her mother was here, sir—I do. Where she has been is more than I ken, but her bed has not been lain on this night."

"She has felt restless, doubtless, and went for a walk, though the hour was certainly a strange one."

Mrs. Adams pursed her lip and shook her head. But then as she stood at the casement, the girl beneath looked smilingly up at her and beckoned to her with a merry gesture to open the window.

"Have you my tea there?" she asked in a rich, clear voice, with a touch of the mincing French accent.

"It is in your room, miss."

"Look at my boots, Mrs. Adams!" she cried, thrusting them out from under her skirt. "These fells of yours are dreadful places—effroyable—one inch, two inch; never have I seen such mud! My dress, too—voilà!"

"Eh, miss, but you are in a pickle," cried the landlady, as she gazed down at the bedraggled gown. "But you must be main weary and heavy for sleep."

"No, no," she answered laughingly, "I care not for sleep. What is sleep? it is a little death—voilà tout. But for me to walk, to run, to breathe the air—that is to live. I was not tired, and so all night I have explored these fells of Yorkshire."

"Lord 'a mercy, miss, and where did you go?" asked Mrs. Adams.

She waved her hand round in a sweeping gesture which included the whole western horizon. "There," she cried. "O comme elles sont tristes et sauvages, ces collines! But I have flowers here. You will give me water, will you not? They will wither else." She gathered her treasures in her lap, and a moment later we heard her light, springy footfall upon the stair.

So she had been out all night, this strange woman. What motive could have taken her from her snug room on to the bleak, wind swept hills? Could it be merely the restlessness, the love of adventure of a young girl? Or was there, possibly, some deeper meaning in this nocturnal journey?

Deep as were the mysteries which my studies had taught me to solve, here was a human problem which for the moment at least was beyond my comprehension. I had walked out on the moor in the forenoon, and on my return, as I topped the brow that overlooks the little town, I saw my fellow-lodger some little distance off amongst the gorse. She had raised a light easel in front of her, and, with papered board laid across it, was preparing to paint the magnificent landscape of rock and moor which stretched away in front of her. As I watched her I saw that she was looking anxiously to right and left. Close by me a pool of water had formed in a hollow. Dipping the cup of my pocket-flask into it, I carried it across to her.

"Miss Cameron, I believe," said I. "I am your fellow-lodger. Upperton is my name. We must introduce ourselves in these wilds if we are not to be for ever strangers."

"Oh, then, you live also with Mrs. Adams!" she cried. "I had thought that there were none but peasants in this strange place."

"I am a visitor, like yourself," I answered. "I am a student, and have come for quiet and repose, which my studies demand."

"Quiet, indeed!" said she, glancing round at the vast circle of silent moors, with the one tiny line of grey cottages which sloped down beneath us.

"And yet not quiet enough," I answered, laughing, "for I have been forced to move further into the fells for the absolute peace which I require."

"Have you, then, built a house upon the fells?" she asked, arching her eyebrows.

"I have, and hope within a few days to occupy it."

"Ah, but that is triste," she cried. "And where is it, then, this house which you have built?"

"It is over yonder," I answered. "See that stream which lies like a silver band upon the distant moor? It is the Gaster Beck, and it runs through Gaster Fell."

She started, and turned upon me her great dark, questioning eyes with a look in which surprise, incredulity, and something akin to horror seemed to be struggling for mastery.

"And you will live on the Gaster Fell?" she cried.

"So I have planned. But what do you know of Gaster Fell, Miss Cameron?" I asked. "I had thought that you were a stranger in these parts."

"Indeed, I have never been here before," she answered. "But I have heard my brother talk of these Yorkshire moors; and, if I mistake not, I have heard him name this very one as the wildest and most savage of them all."

"Very likely," said I carelessly. "It is indeed a dreary place."

"Then why live there?" she cried eagerly. "Consider the loneliness, the barrenness, the want of all comfort and of all aid, should aid be needed."

"Aid! What aid should be needed on Gaster Fell?"

She looked down and shrugged her shoulders. "Sickness may come in all places," said she. "If I were a man I do not think I would live alone on Gaster Fell."

"I have braved worse dangers than that," said I, laughing; "but I fear that your picture will be spoiled, for the clouds are banking up, and already I feel a few raindrops."

Indeed, it was high time we were on our way to shelter, for even as I spoke there came the sudden, steady swish of the shower. Laughing merrily, my companion threw her light shawl over her head, and, seizing picture and easel, ran with the lithe grace of a young fawn down the furze-clad slope, while I followed after with camp-stool and paint-box.

It was the eve of my departure from Kirkby-Malhouse that we sat upon the green bank in the garden, she with dark, dreamy eyes looking sadly out over the sombre fells; while I, with a book upon my knee, glanced covertly at her lovely profile and marvelled to myself how twenty years of life could have stamped so sad and wistful an expression upon it.

"You have read much," I remarked at last. "Women have opportunities now such as their mothers never knew. Have you ever thought of going further—of seeking a course of college or even a learned profession?"

She smiled wearily at the thought.

"I have no aim, no ambition," she said. "My future is black—confused—a chaos. My life is like to one of these paths upon the fells. You have seen them, Monsieur Upperton. They are smooth and straight and clear where they begin; but soon they wind to left and wind to right, and so mid rocks and crags until they lose themselves in some quagmire. At Brussels my path was straight; but now, mon Dieu! who is there can tell me where it leads?"

"It might take no prophet to do that, Miss Cameron," quoth I, with the fatherly manner which two-score years may show toward one. "If I may read your life, I would venture to say that you were destined to fulfil the lot of women—to make some good man happy, and to shed around, in some wider circle, the pleasure which your society has given me since first I knew you."

"I will never marry," said she, with a sharp decision, which surprised and somewhat amused me.

"Not marry—and why?"

A strange look passed over her sensitive features, and she plucked nervously at the grass on the bank beside her.

"I dare not," said she in a voice that quivered with emotion.

"Dare not?"

"It is not for me. I have other things to do. That path of which I spoke is one which I must tread alone."

"But this is morbid," said I. "Why should your lot, Miss Cameron, be separated from that of my own sisters, or the thousand other young ladies whom every season brings out into the world? But perhaps it is that you have a fear and distrust of mankind. Marriage brings a risk as well as a happiness."

"The risk would be with the man who married me," she cried. And then in an instant, as though she had said too much, she sprang to her feet and drew her mantle round her. "The night air is chill, Mr. Upperton," said she, and so swept swiftly away, leaving me to muse over the strange words which had fallen from her lips.

Clearly, it was time that I should go. I set my teeth and vowed that another day should not have passed before I should have snapped this newly formed tie and sought the lonely retreat which awaited me upon the moors. Breakfast was hardly over in the morning before a peasant dragged up to the door the rude hand-cart which was to convey my few personal belongings to my new dwelling. My fellow-lodger had kept her room; and, steeled as my mind was against her influence, I was yet conscious of a little throb of disappointment that she should allow me to depart without a word of farewell. My hand-cart with its load of books had already started, and I, having shaken hands with Mrs. Adams, was about to follow it, when there was a quick scurry of feet on the stair, and there she was beside me all panting with her own haste.

"Then you go—you really go?" said she.

"My studies call me."

"And to Gaster Fell?" she asked.

"Yes; to the cottage which I have built there."

"And you will live alone there?"

"With my hundred companions who lie in that cart."

"Ah, books!" she cried, with a pretty shrug of her graceful shoulders. "But you will make me a promise?"

"What is it?" I asked, in surprise.

"It is a small thing. You will not refuse me?"

"You have but to ask it."

She bent forward her beautiful face with an expression of the most intense earnestness. "You will bolt your door at night?" said she; and was gone ere I could say a word in answer to her extraordinary request.

It was a strange thing for me to find myself at last duly installed in my lonely dwelling. For me, now, the horizon was bounded by the barren circle of wiry, unprofitable grass, patched over with furze bushes and scarred by the profusion of Nature's gaunt and granite ribs. A duller, wearier waste I have never seen; but its dulness was its very charm.

And yet the very first night which I spent at Gaster Fell there came a strange incident to lead my thoughts back once more to the world which I had left behind me.

It had been a sullen and sultry evening, with great livid cloud-banks mustering in the west. As the night wore on, the air within my little cabin became closer and more oppressive. A weight seemed to rest upon my brow and my chest. From far away the low rumble of thunder came moaning over the moor. Unable to sleep, I dressed, and standing at my cottage door, looked on the black solitude which surrounded me.

Taking the narrow sheep path which ran by this stream, I strolled along it for some hundred yards, and had turned to retrace my steps, when the moon was finally buried beneath an ink-black cloud, and the darkness deepened so suddenly that I could see neither the path at my feet, the stream upon my right, nor the rocks upon my left. I was standing groping about in the thick gloom, when there came a crash of thunder with a flash of lightning which lighted up the whole vast fell, so that every bush and rock stood out clear and hard in the vivid light. It was but for an instant, and yet that momentary view struck a thrill of fear and astonishment through me, for in my very path, not twenty yards before me, there stood a woman, the livid light beating upon her face and showing up every detail of her dress and features.

There was no mistaking those dark eyes, that tall, graceful figure. It was she—Eva Cameron, the woman whom I thought I had for ever left. For an instant I stood petrified, marvelling whether this could indeed be she, or whether it was some figment conjured up by my excited brain. Then I ran swiftly forward in the direction where I had seen her, calling loudly upon her, but without reply. Again I called, and again no answer came back, save the melancholy wail of the owl. A second flash illuminated the landscape, and the moon burst out from behind its cloud. But I could not, though I climbed upon a knoll which overlooked the whole moor, see any sign of this strange midnight wanderer. For an hour or more I traversed the fell, and at last found myself back at my little cabin, still uncertain as to whether it had been a woman or a shadow upon which I gazed.

III: OF THE GREY COTTAGE IN THE GLEN

It was either on the fourth or the fifth day after I had taken possession of my cottage that I was astonished to hear footsteps upon the grass outside, quickly followed by a crack, as from a stick upon the door. The explosion of an infernal machine would hardly have surprised or discomfited me more. I had hoped to have shaken off all intrusion for ever, yet here was somebody beating at my door with as little ceremony as if it had been a village ale-house. Hot with anger, I flung down my book and withdrew the bolt just as my visitor had raised his stick to renew his rough application for admittance. He was a tall, powerful man, tawny-bearded and deep-chested, clad in a loose-fitting suit of tweed, cut for comfort rather than elegance. As he stood in the shimmering sunlight, I took in every feature of his face. The large, fleshy nose; the steady blue eyes, with their thick thatch of overhanging brows; the broad forehead, all knitted and lined with furrows, which were strangely at variance with his youthful bearing. In spite of his weather-stained felt hat, and the coloured handkerchief slung round his muscular brown neck, I could see at a glance he was a man of breeding and education. I had been prepared for some wandering shepherd or uncouth tramp, but this apparition fairly disconcerted me.

"You look astonished," said he, with a smile. "Did you think, then, that you were the only man in the world with a taste for solitude? You see that there are other hermits in the wilderness besides yourself."

"Do you mean to say that you live here?" I asked in no conciliatory voice.

"Up yonder," he answered, tossing his head backward. "I thought as we were neighbours, Mr. Upperton, that I could not do less than look in and see if I could assist you in any way."

"Thank you," I said coldly, standing with my hand upon the latch of the door. "I am a man of simple tastes, and you can do nothing for me. You have the advantage of me in knowing my name."

He appeared to be chilled by my ungracious manner.

"I learned it from the masons who were at work here," he said. "As for me, I am a surgeon, the surgeon of Gaster Fell. That is the name I have gone by in these parts, and it serves as well as another."

"Not much room for practice here?" I observed.

"Not a soul except yourself for miles on either side."

"You appear to have had need of some assistance yourself," I remarked, glancing at a broad white splash, as from the recent action of some powerful acid, upon his sunburnt cheek.

"That is nothing," he answered, curtly, turning his face half round to hide the mark. "I must get back, for I have a companion who is waiting for me. If I can ever do anything for you, pray let me know. You have only to follow the beck upward for a mile or so to find my place. Have you a bolt on the inside of your door?"

"Yes," I answered, rather startled at this question.

"Keep it bolted, then," he said. "The fell is a strange place. You never know who may be about. It is as well to be on the safe side.

Good-bye." He raised his hat, turned on his heel and lounged away along the bank of the little stream.

I was still standing with my hand upon the latch, gazing after my unexpected visitor, when I became aware of yet another dweller in the wilderness. Some distance along the path which the stranger was taking there lay a great grey boulder, and leaning against this was a small, wizened man, who stood erect as the other approached, and advanced to meet him. The two talked for a minute or more, the taller man nodding his head frequently in my direction, as though describing what had passed between us. Then they walked on together, and disappeared in a dip of the fell. Presently I saw them ascending once more some rising ground farther on. My acquaintance had thrown his arm round his elderly friend, either from affection or from a desire to aid him up the steep incline. The square burly figure and its shrivelled, meagre companion stood out against the sky-line, and turning their faces, they looked back at me. At the sight, I slammed the door, lest they should be encouraged to return. But when I peeped from the window some minutes afterward, I perceived that they were gone.

All day I bent over the Egyptian papyrus upon which I was engaged; but neither the subtle reasonings of the ancient philosopher of Memphis, nor the mystic meaning which lay in his pages, could raise my mind from the things of earth. Evening was drawing in before I threw my work aside in despair. My heart was bitter against this man for his intrusion. Standing by the beck which purled past the door of my cabin, I cooled my heated brow, and thought the matter over. Clearly it was the small mystery hanging over these neighbours of mine which had caused my mind to run so persistently on them. That cleared up, they would no longer cause an obstacle to my studies. What was to hinder me, then, from walking in the direction of their dwelling, and observing for myself, without permitting them to suspect my presence, what manner of men they might be? Doubtless, their mode of life would be found to admit of some simple and prosaic explanation. In any case, the evening was fine, and a walk would be bracing for mind and body. Lighting my pipe, I set off over the moors in the direction which they had taken.

About half-way down a wild glen there stood a small clump of gnarled and stunted oak trees. From behind these, a thin dark column of smoke rose into the still evening air. Clearly this marked the position of my neighbour's house. Trending away to the left, I was able to gain the shelter of a line of rocks, and so reach a spot from which I could command a view of the building without exposing myself to any risk of being observed. It was a small, slate-covered cottage, hardly larger than the boulders among which it lay. Like my own cabin, it showed signs of having been constructed for the use of some shepherd; but, unlike mine, no pains had been taken by the tenants to improve and enlarge it. Two little peeping windows, a cracked and weather-beaten door, and a discoloured barrel for catching the rain water, were the only external objects from which I might draw deductions as to the dwellers within. Yet even in these there was food for thought, for as I drew nearer, still concealing myself behind the ridge, I saw that thick bars of iron covered the windows, while the old door was slashed and plated with the same metal. These strange precautions, together with the wild surroundings and unbroken solitude, gave an indescribably ill omen and fearsome character to the solitary building. Thrusting my pipe into my pocket, I crawled upon my hands and knees through the gorse and ferns until I was within a hundred yards of my neighbour's door. There, finding that I could not approach nearer without fear of detection, I crouched down, and set myself to watch.

I had hardly settled into my hiding place, when the door of the cottage swung open, and the man who had introduced himself to me as the surgeon of Gaster Fell came out, bareheaded, with a spade in his hands. In front of the door there was a small cultivated patch containing potatoes, peas and other forms of green stuff, and here he proceeded to busy himself, trimming, weeding and arranging, singing the while in a powerful though not very musical voice. He was all engrossed in his work, with his back to the cottage, when there emerged from the half-open door the same attenuated creature whom I had seen in the morning. I could perceive now that he was a man of sixty, wrinkled, bent, and feeble, with sparse, grizzled hair, and long, colourless face. With a cringing, sidelong gait, he shuffled toward his companion, who was unconscious of his approach until he was close upon him. His light footfall or his breathing may have finally given notice of his proximity, for the worker sprang round and faced him. Each made a quick step toward the other, as though in greeting, and then—even now I feel the horror of the instant—the tall man rushed upon and knocked his companion to the earth, then whipping up his body, ran with great speed over the intervening ground and disappeared with his burden into the house.

Case hardened as I was by my varied life, the suddenness and violence of the thing made me shudder. The man's age, his feeble frame, his humble and deprecating manner, all cried shame against the deed. So hot was my anger, that I was on the point of striding up to the cabin, unarmed as I was, when the sound of voices from within showed me that the victim had recovered. The sun had sunk beneath the horizon, and all was grey, save a red feather in the cap of Pennigent. Secure in the failing light, I approached near and strained my ears to catch what was passing. I could hear the high, querulous voice of the elder man and the deep, rough monotone of his assailant, mixed with a strange metallic jangling and clanking. Presently the surgeon came out, locked the door behind him and stamped up and down in the twilight, pulling at his hair and brandishing his arms, like a man demented. Then he set off, walking rapidly up the valley, and I soon lost sight of him among the rocks.

When his footsteps had died away in the distance, I drew nearer to the cottage. The prisoner within was still pouring forth a stream of words, and moaning from time to time like a man in pain. These words resolved themselves, as I approached, into prayers—shrill, voluble prayers, pattered forth with the intense earnestness of one who sees impending and imminent danger. There was to me something inexpressibly awesome in this gush of solemn entreaty from the lonely sufferer, meant for no human ear, and jarring upon the silence of the night. I was still pondering whether I should mix myself in the affair or not, when I heard in the distance the sound of the surgeon's returning footfall. At that I drew myself up quickly by the iron bars and glanced in through the diamond-paned window. The interior of the cottage was lighted up by a lurid glow, coming from what I afterward discovered to be a chemical furnace. By its rich light I could distinguish a great litter of retorts, test tubes and condensers, which sparkled over the table, and threw strange, grotesque shadows on the wall. On the further side of the room was a wooden framework resembling a hencoop, and in this, still absorbed in prayer, knelt the man whose voice I heard. The red glow beating upon his upturned face made it stand out from the shadow like a painting from Rembrandt, showing up every wrinkle upon the parchment-like skin. I had but time for a fleeting glance; then, dropping from the window, I made off through the rocks and the heather, nor slackened my pace until I found myself back in my cabin once more. There I threw myself upon my couch, more disturbed and shaken than I had ever thought to feel again.

Such doubts as I might have had as to whether I had indeed seen my former fellow-lodger upon the night of the thunderstorm were resolved the next morning. Strolling along down the path which led to the fell, I saw in one spot where the ground was soft the impressions of a foot—the small, dainty foot of a well-booted woman. That tiny heel and high in-step could have belonged to none other than my companion of Kirkby-Malhouse. I followed her trail for some distance, till it still pointed, so far as I could discern it, to the lonely and ill-omened cottage. What power could there be to draw this tender girl, through wind and rain and darkness, across the fearsome moors to that strange rendezvous?

I have said that a little beck flowed down the valley and past my very door. A week or so after the doings which I have described, I was seated by my window when I perceived something white drifting slowly down the stream. My first thought was that it was a drowning sheep; but picking up my stick, I strolled to the bank and hooked it ashore. On examination it prove to be a large sheet, torn and tattered, with the initials J. C. in the corner. What gave it its sinister significance, however, was that from hem to hem it was all dabbled and discoloured.

Shutting the door of my cabin, I set off up the glen in the direction of the surgeon's cabin. I had not gone far before I perceived the very man himself. He was walking rapidly along the hillside, beating the furze bushes with a cudgel and bellowing like a madman. Indeed, at the sight of him, the doubts as to his sanity which had risen in my mind were strengthened and confirmed.

As he approached I noticed that his left arm was suspended in a sling. On perceiving me he stood irresolute, as though uncertain whether to come over to me or not. I had no desire for an interview with him, however, so I hurried past him, on which he continued on his way, still shouting and striking about with his club. When he had disappeared over the fells, I made my way down to his cottage, determined to find some clue to what occurred. I was surprised, on reaching it, to find the iron-plated door flung wide open. The ground immediately outside it was marked with the signs of a struggle. The chemical apparatus within and the furniture were all dashed about and shattered. Most suggestive of all, the sinister wooden cage was stained with blood-marks, and its unfortunate occupant had disappeared. My heart was heavy for the little man, for I was assured I should never see him in this world more.

There was nothing in the cabin to throw any light upon the identity of my neighbours. The room was stuffed with chemical instruments. In one corner a small bookcase contained a choice selection of works of science. In another was a pile of geological specimens collected from the limestone.

I caught no glimpse of the surgeon upon my homeward journey; but when I reached my cottage I was astonished and indignant to find that somebody had entered it in my absence. Boxes had been pulled out from under the bed, the curtains disarranged, the chairs drawn out from the wall. Even my study had not been safe from this rough intruder, for the prints of a heavy boot were plainly visible on the ebony-black carpet.

IV: OF THE MAN WHO CAME IN THE NIGHT

The night set in gusty and tempestuous, and the moon was all girt with ragged clouds. The wind blew in melancholy gusts, sobbing and sighing over the moor, and setting all the gorse bushes agroaning. From time to time a little sputter of rain pattered up against the window-pane. I sat until near midnight, glancing over the fragment on immortality by Iamblichus, the Alexandrian platonist, of whom the Emperor Julian said that he was posterior to Plato in time but not in genius. At last, shutting up my book, I opened my door and took a last look at the dreary fell and still more dreary sky. As I protruded my head, a swoop of wind caught me and sent the red ashes of my pipe sparkling and dancing through the darkness. At the same moment the moon shone brilliantly out from between two clouds and I saw, sitting on the hillside, not two hundred yards from my door, the man who called himself the surgeon of Gaster Fell. He was squatted among the heather, his elbows upon his knees, and his chin resting upon his hands, as motionless as a stone, with his gaze fixed steadily upon the door of my dwelling.

At the sight of this ill-omened sentinel, a chill of horror and of fear shot through me, for his gloomy and mysterious associations had cast a glamour round the man, and the hour and place were in keeping with his sinister presence. In a moment, however, a manly glow of resentment and self-confidence drove this petty emotion from my mind, and I strode fearlessly in his direction. He rose as I approached and faced me, with the moon shining on his grave, bearded face and glittering on his eyeballs. "What is the meaning of this?" I cried, as I came upon him. "What right have you to play the spy on me?"

I could see the flush of anger rise on his face. "Your stay in the country has made you forget your manners," he said. "The moor is free to all."

"You will say next that my house is free to all," I said, hotly. "You have had the impertinence to ransack it in my absence this afternoon."

He started, and his features showed the most intense excitement. "I swear to you that I had no hand in it!" he cried. "I have never set foot in your house in my life. Oh, sir, sir, if you will but believe me, there is a danger hanging over you, and you would do well to be careful."

"I have had enough of you," I said. "I saw that cowardly blow you struck when you thought no human eye rested upon you. I have been to your cottage, too, and know all that it has to tell. If there is a law in England, you shall hang for what you have done. As to me, I am an old soldier, sir, and I am armed. I shall not fasten my door. But if you or any other villain attempt to cross my threshold it shall be at your own risk." With these words, I swung round upon my heel and strode into my cabin.

For two days the wind freshened and increased, with constant squalls of rain until on the third night the most furious storm was raging which I can ever recollect in England. I felt that it was positively useless to go to bed, nor could I concentrate my mind sufficiently to read a book. I turned my lamp half down to moderate the glare, and leaning back in my chair, I gave myself up to reverie. I must have lost all perception of time, for I have no recollection how long I sat there on the borderland betwixt thought and slumber. At last, about 3 or possibly 4 o'clock, I came to myself with a start—not only came to myself, but with every sense and nerve upon the strain. Looking round my chamber in the dim light, I could not see anything to justify my sudden trepidation. The homely room, the rain-blurred window and the rude wooden door were all as they had been. I had begun to persuade myself that some half-formed dream had sent that vague thrill through my nerves, when in a moment I became conscious of what it was. It was a sound—the sound of a human step outside my solitary cottage.

Amid the thunder and the rain and the wind I could hear it—a dull, stealthy footfall, now on the grass, now on the stones—occasionally stopping entirely, then resumed, and ever drawing nearer. I sat breathlessly, listening to the eerie sound. It had stopped now at my very door, and was replaced by a panting and gasping, as of one who has travelled fast and far.

By the flickering light of the expiring lamp I could see that the latch of my door was twitching, as though a gentle pressure was exerted on it from without. Slowly, slowly, it rose, until it was free of the catch, and then there was a pause of a quarter minute or more, while I still sat silent with dilated eyes and drawn sabre. Then, very slowly, the door began to revolve upon its hinges, and the keen air of the night came whistling through the slit. Very cautiously it was pushed open, so that never a sound came from the rusty hinges. As the aperture enlarged, I became aware of a dark, shadowy figure upon my threshold, and of a pale face that looked in at me. The features were human, but the eyes were not. They seemed to burn through the darkness with a greenish brilliancy of their own; and in their baleful, shifty glare I was conscious of the very spirit of murder. Springing from my chair, I had raised my naked sword, when, with a wild shouting, a second figure dashed up to my door. At its approach my shadowy visitant uttered a shrill cry, and fled away across the fells, yelping like a beaten hound.

Tingling with my recent fear, I stood at my door, peering through the night with the discordant cry of the fugitives still ringing in my ears. At that moment a vivid flash of lightning illuminated the whole landscape and made it as clear as day. By its light I saw far away upon the hillside two dark figures pursuing each other with extreme rapidity across the fells. Even at that distance the contrast between them forbid all doubt as to their identity. The first was the small, elderly man, whom I had supposed to be dead; the second was my neighbour, the surgeon. For an instant they stood out clear and hard in the unearthly light; in the next, the darkness had closed over them, and they were gone. As I turned to re-enter my chamber, my foot rattled against something on my threshold. Stooping, I found it was a straight knife, fashioned entirely of lead, and so soft and brittle that it was a strange choice for a weapon. To render it more harmless, the top had been cut square off. The edge, however, had been assiduously sharpened against a stone, as was evident from the markings upon it, so that it was still a dangerous implement in the grasp of a determined man.

And what was the meaning of it all? you ask. Many a drama which I have come across in my wandering life, some as strange and as striking as this one, has lacked the ultimate explanation which you demand. Fate is a grand weaver of tales; but she ends them, as a rule, in defiance of all artistic laws, and with an unbecoming want of regard for literary propriety. As it happens, however, I have a letter before me as I write which I may add without comment, and which will clear all that may remain dark.

"Kirkby Lunatic Asylum,

"September 4th, 1885.

"Sir,—I am deeply conscious that some apology and explanation is due to you for the very startling and, in your eyes, mysterious events which have recently occurred, and which have so seriously interfered with the retired existence which you desire to lead. I should have called upon you on the morning after the recapture of my father, but my knowledge of your dislike to visitors and also of— you will excuse my saying it—your very violent temper, led me to think that it was better to communicate with you by letter.

"My poor father was a hard-working general practitioner in Birmingham, where his name is still remembered and respected. About ten years ago he began to show signs of mental aberration, which we were inclined to put down to overwork and the effects of a sunstroke. Feeling my own incompetence to pronounce upon a case of such importance, I at once sought the highest advice in Birmingham and London. Among others we consulted the eminent alienist, Mr. Fraser Brown, who pronounced my father's case to be intermittent in its nature, but dangerous during the paroxysms. 'It may take a homicidal, or it may take a religious turn,' he said; 'or it may prove to be a mixture of both. For months he may be as well as you or I, and then in a moment he may break out. You will incur a great responsibility if you leave him without supervision.'

"I need say no more, sir. You will understand the terrible task which has fallen upon my poor sister and me in endeavoring to save my father from the asylum which in his sane moments filled him with horror. I can only regret that your peace has been disturbed by our misfortunes, and I offer you in my sister's name and my own our apologies.

"Yours truly,

"J. Cameron."

III

BORROWED SCENES

"It cannot be done. People really would not stand it. I know because I have tried."—Extract from an unpublished paper upon George Borrow and his writings.

Yes, I tried and my experience may interest other people. You must imagine, then, that I am soaked in George Borrow, especially in his Lavengro and his Romany Rye, that I have modelled both my thoughts, my speech and my style very carefully upon those of the master, and that finally I set forth one summer day actually to lead the life of which I had read. Behold me, then, upon the country road which leads from the railway-station to the Sussex village of Swinehurst.

As I walked, I entertained myself by recollections of the founders of Sussex, of Cerdic that mighty sea-rover, and of Ella his son, said by the bard to be taller by the length of a spear-head than the tallest of his fellows. I mentioned the matter twice to peasants whom I met upon the road. One, a tallish man with a freckled face, sidled past me and ran swiftly towards the station. The other, a smaller and older man, stood entranced while I recited to him that passage of the Saxon Chronicle which begins, "Then came Leija with longships forty-four, and the fyrd went out against him." I was pointing out to him that the Chronicle had been written partly by the monks of Saint Albans and afterwards by those of Peterborough, but the fellow sprang suddenly over a gate and disappeared.

The village of Swinehurst is a straggling line of half-timbered houses of the early English pattern. One of these houses stood, as I observed, somewhat taller than the rest, and seeing by its appearance and by the sign which hung before it that it was the village inn, I approached it, for indeed I had not broken my fast since I had left London. A stoutish man, five foot eight perhaps in height, with black coat and trousers of a greyish shade, stood outside, and to him I talked in the fashion of the master.

"Why a rose and why a crown?" I asked as I pointed upwards.

He looked at me in a strange manner. The man's whole appearance was strange. "Why not?" he answered, and shrank a little backwards.

"The sign of a king," said I.

"Surely," said he. "What else should we understand from a crown?"

"And which king?" I asked.

"You will excuse me," said he, and tried to pass.

"Which king?" I repeated.

"How should I know?" he asked.

"You should know by the rose," said I, "which is the symbol of that Tudor-ap-Tudor, who, coming from the mountains of Wales, yet seated his posterity upon the English throne. Tudor," I continued, getting between the stranger and the door of the inn, through which he appeared to be desirous of passing, "was of the same blood as Owen Glendower, the famous chieftain, who is by no means to be confused with Owen Gwynedd, the father of Madoc of the Sea, of whom the bard made the famous cnylyn, which runs in the Welsh as follows:—"

I was about to repeat the famous stanza of Dafydd-ap-Gwilyn when the man, who had looked very fixedly and strangely at me as I spoke, pushed past me and entered the inn. "Truly," said I aloud, "it is surely Swinehurst to which I have come, since the same means the grove of the hogs." So saying I followed the fellow into the bar parlour, where I perceived him seated in a corner with a large chair in front of him. Four persons of various degrees were drinking beer at a central table, whilst a small man of active build, in a black, shiny suit, which seemed to have seen much service, stood before the empty fireplace. Him I took to be the landlord, and I asked him what I should have for my dinner.

He smiled, and said that he could not tell.

"But surely, my friend," said I, "you can tell me what is ready?"

"Even that I cannot do," he answered; "but I doubt not that the landlord can inform us." On this he rang the bell, and a fellow answered, to whom I put the same question.

"What would you have?" he asked.

I thought of the master, and I ordered a cold leg of pork to be washed down with tea and beer.

"Did you say tea and beer?" asked the landlord.

"I did."

"For twenty-five years have I been in business," said the landlord, "and never before have I been asked for tea and beer."

"The gentleman is joking," said the man with the shining coat.

"Or else——" said the elderly man in the corner.

"Or what, sir?" I asked.

"Nothing," said he—"nothing." There was something very strange in this man in the corner—him to whom I had spoken of Dafydd-ap-Gwilyn.

"Then you are joking," said the landlord.

I asked him if he had read the works of my master, George Borrow. He said that he had not. I told him that in those five volumes he would not, from cover to cover, find one trace of any sort of a joke. He would also find that my master drank tea and beer together. Now it happens that about tea I have read nothing either in the sagas or in the bardic cnylynions, but, whilst the landlord had departed to prepare my meal, I recited to the company those Icelandic stanzas which praise the beer of Gunnar, the long-haired son of Harold the Bear. Then, lest the language should be unknown to some of them, I recited my own translation, ending with the line—

"If the beer be small, then let the mug be large."

I then asked the company whether they went to church or to chapel. The question surprised them, and especially the strange man in the corner, upon whom I now fixed my eye. I had read his secret, and as I looked at him he tried to shrink behind the clock-case.

"The church or the chapel?" I asked him.

"The church," he gasped.

"Which church?" I asked.

He shrank farther behind the clock. "I have never been so questioned," he cried.

I showed him that I knew his secret. "Rome was not built in a day," said I.

"He! He!" he cried. Then, as I turned away, he put his head from behind the clock-case, and tapped his forehead with his fore-finger. So also did the man with the shiny coat, who stood before the empty fireplace.

Having eaten the cold leg of pork—where is there a better dish, save only boiled mutton with capers?—and having drunk both the tea and the beer, I told the company that such a meal had been called "to box Harry" by the master, who had observed it to be in great favour with commercial gentlemen out of Liverpool. With this information and a stanza or two from Lopez de Vega I left the Inn of the Rose and Crown behind me, having first paid my reckoning. At the door the landlord asked me for my name and address.

"And why?" I asked.

"Lest there should be inquiry for you," said the landlord.

"But why should they enquire for me?"

"Ah, who knows?" said the landlord, musing. And so I left him at the door of the Inn of the Rose and Crown, whence came, I observed, a great tumult of laughter. "Assuredly," thought I, "Rome was not built in a day."

Having walked down the main street of Swinehurst, which, as I have observed, consists of half-timbered buildings in the ancient style, I came out upon the country road, and proceeded to look for those wayside adventures, which are, according to the master, as thick as blackberries for those who seek them upon an English highway. I had already received some boxing lessons before leaving London, so it seemed to me that if I should chance to meet some traveller whose size and age seemed such as to encourage the venture, I would ask him to strip off his coat and settle any differences which we could find in the old English fashion. I waited, therefore, by a stile for any one who should chance to pass, and it was while I stood there that the screaming horror came upon me, even as it came upon the master in the dingle. I gripped the bar of the stile, which was of good British oak. Oh, who can tell the terrors of the screaming horror! That was what I thought as I grasped the oaken bar of the stile. Was it the beer—or was it the tea? Or was it that the landlord was right and that other, the man with the black, shiny coat, he who had answered the sign of the strange man in the corner? But the master drank tea with beer. Yes, but the master also had the screaming horror. All this I thought as I grasped the bar of British oak, which was the top of the stile. For half an hour the horror was upon me. Then it passed, and I was left feeling very weak and still grasping the oaken bar.

I had not moved from the stile, where I had been seized by the screaming horror, when I heard the sound of steps behind me, and turning round I perceived that a pathway led across the field upon the farther side of the stile. A woman was coming towards me along this pathway, and it was evident to me that she was one of those gipsy Rias, of whom the master has said so much. Looking beyond her, I could see the smoke of a fire from a small dingle, which showed where her tribe were camping. The woman herself was of a moderate height, neither tall nor short, with a face which was much sunburned and freckled. I must confess that she was not beautiful, but I do not think that any one, save the master, has found very beautiful women walking about upon the high-roads of England. Such as she was I must make the best of her, and well I knew how to address her, for many times had I admired the mixture of politeness and audacity which should be used in such a case. Therefore, when the woman had come to the stile, I held out my hand and helped her over.

"What says the Spanish poet Calderon?" said I. "I doubt not that you have read the couplet which has been thus Englished:

'Oh, maiden, may I humbly pray

That I may help you on your way.'"

The woman blushed, but said nothing.

"Where," I asked, "are the Romany chals and the Romany chis?"

She turned her head away and was silent.

"Though I am a gorgio," said I, "I know something of the Romany lil," and to prove it I sang the stanza—

"Coliko, coliko saulo wer

Apopli to the farming ker

Will wel and mang him mullo,

Will wel and mang his truppo."

The girl laughed, but said nothing. It appeared to me from her appearance that she might be one of those who make a living at telling fortunes or "dukkering," as the master calls it, at racecourses and other gatherings of the sort.

"Do you dukker?" I asked.

She slapped me on the arm. "Well, you are a pot of ginger!" said she.

I was pleased at the slap, for it put me in mind of the peerless Belle. "You can use Long Melford," said I, an expression which, with the master, meant fighting.

"Get along with your sauce!" said she, and struck me again.

"You are a very fine young woman," said I, "and remind me of Grunelda, the daughter of Hjalmar, who stole the golden bowl from the King of the Islands."

She seemed annoyed at this. "You keep a civil tongue, young man," said she.

"I meant no harm, Belle. I was but comparing you to one of whom the saga says her eyes were like the shine of sun upon icebergs."

This seemed to please her, for she smiled. "My name ain't Belle," she said at last.

"What is your name?"

"Henrietta."

"The name of a queen," I said aloud.

"Go on," said the girl.

"Of Charles's queen," said I, "of whom Waller the poet (for the English also have their poets, though in this respect far inferior to the Basques)—of whom, I say, Waller the poet said:

'That she was Queen was the Creator's act,

Belated man could but endorse the fact.'"

"I say!" cried the girl. "How you do go on!"

"So now," said I, "since I have shown you that you are a queen you will surely give me a choomer"—this being a kiss in Romany talk.

"I'll give you one on the ear-hole," she cried.

"Then I will wrestle with you," said I. "If you should chance to put me down, I will do penance by teaching you the Armenian alphabet—the very word alphabet, as you will perceive, shows us that our letters came from Greece. If, on the other hand, I should chance to put you down, you will give me a choomer."

I had got so far, and she was climbing the stile with some pretence of getting away from me, when there came a van along the road, belonging, as I discovered, to a baker in Swinehurst. The horse, which was of a brown colour, was such as is bred in the New Forest, being somewhat under fifteen hands and of a hairy, ill-kempt variety. As I know less than the master about horses, I will say no more of this horse, save to repeat that its colour was brown—nor indeed had the horse nor the horse's colour anything to do with my narrative. I might add, however, that it could either be taken as a small horse or as a large pony, being somewhat tall for the one, but undersized for the other. I have now said enough about this horse, which has nothing to do with my story, and I will turn my attention to the driver.

This was a man with a broad, florid face and brown side-whiskers. He was of a stout build and had rounded shoulders, with a small mole of a reddish colour over his left eyebrow. His jacket was of velveteen, and he had large, iron shod boots, which were perched upon the splashboard in front of him. He pulled up the van as he came up to the stile near which I was standing with the maiden who had come from the dingle, and in a civil fashion he asked me if I could oblige him with a light for his pipe. Then, as I drew a matchbox from my pocket, he threw his reins over the splashboard, and removing his large, iron-shod boots he descended on to the road. He was a burly man, but inclined to fat and scant of breath. It seemed to me that it was a chance for one of those wayside boxing adventures which were so common in the olden times. It was my intention that I should fight the man, and that the maiden from the dingle standing by me should tell me when to use my right or my left, as the case might be, picking me up also in case I should be so unfortunate as to be knocked down by the man with the iron-shod boots and the small mole of a reddish colour over his left eyebrow.

"Do you use Long Melford?" I asked.

He looked at me in some surprise, and said that any mixture was good enough for him.

"By Long Melford," said I, "I do not mean, as you seem to think, some form of tobacco, but I mean that art and science of boxing which was held in such high esteem by our ancestors, that some famous professors of it, such as the great Gully, have been elected to the highest offices of the State. There were men of the highest character amongst the bruisers of England, of whom I would particularly mention Tom of Hereford, better known as Tom Spring, though his father's name, as I have been given to understand, was Winter. This, however, has nothing to do with the matter in hand, which is that you must fight me."

The man with the florid face seemed very much surprised at my words, so that I cannot think that adventures of this sort were as common as I had been led by the master to expect.

"Fight!" said he. "What about?"

"It is a good old English custom," said I, "by which we may determine which is the better man."

"I've nothing against you," said he.

"Nor I against you," I answered. "So that we will fight for love, which was an expression much used in olden days. It is narrated by Harold Sygvynson that among the Danes it was usual to do so even with battle-axes, as is told in his second set of runes. Therefore you will take off your coat and fight." As I spoke, I stripped off my own.

The man's face was less florid than before. "I'm not going to fight," said he.

"Indeed you are," I answered, "and this young woman will doubtless do you the service to hold your coat."

"You're clean balmy," said Henrietta.

"Besides," said I, "if you will not fight me for love, perhaps you will fight me for this," and I held out a sovereign. "Will you hold his coat?" I said to Henrietta.

"I'll hold the thick 'un," said she.

"No, you don't," said the man, and put the sovereign into the pocket of his trousers, which were of a corduroy material. "Now," said he, "what am I do to earn this?"

"Fight," said I.

"How do you do it?" he asked.

"Put up your hands," I answered.

He put them up as I had said, and stood there in a sheepish manner with no idea of anything further. It seemed to me that if I could make him angry he would do better, so I knocked off his hat, which was black and hard, of the kind which is called billy-cock.

"Heh, guv'nor!" he cried, "what are you up to?"

"That was to make you angry," said I.

"Well, I am angry," said he.

"Then here is your hat," said I, "and afterwards we shall fight."

I turned as I spoke to pick up his hat, which had rolled behind where I was standing. As I stooped to reach it, I received such a blow that I could neither rise erect nor yet sit down. This blow which I received as I stooped for his billy-cock hat was not from his fist, but from his iron-shod boot, the same which I had observed upon the splashboard. Being unable either to rise erect or yet to sit down, I leaned upon the oaken bar of the stile and groaned loudly on account of the pain of the blow which I had received. Even the screaming horror had given me less pain than this blow from the iron-shod boot. When at last I was able to stand erect, I found that the florid-faced man had driven away with his cart, which could no longer be seen. The maiden from the dingle was standing at the other side of the stile, and a ragged man was running across the field from the direction of the fire.

"Why did you not warn me, Henrietta?" I asked.

"I hadn't time," said she. "Why were you such a chump as to turn your back on him like that?"

The ragged man had reached us, where I stood talking to Henrietta by the stile. I will not try to write his conversation as he said it, because I have observed that the master never condescends to dialect, but prefers by a word introduced here and there to show the fashion of a man's speech. I will only say that the man from the dingle spoke as did the Anglo-Saxons who were wont, as is clearly shown by the venerable Bede, to call their leaders 'Enjist and 'Orsa, two words which in their proper meaning signify a horse and a mare.

"What did he hit you for?" asked the man from the dingle. He was exceedingly ragged, with a powerful frame, a lean brown face, and an oaken cudgel in his hand. His voice was very hoarse and rough, as is the case with those who live in the open air. "The bloke hit you," said he. "What did the bloke hit you for?"

"He asked him to," said Henrietta.

"Asked him to—asked him what?"

"Why, he asked him to hit him. Gave him a thick 'un to do it."

The ragged man seemed surprised. "See here, guv'nor," said he. "If you're collectin', I could let you have one half-price."

"He took me unawares," said I.

"What else would the bloke do when you bashed his hat?" said the maiden from the dingle.

By this time I was able to straighten myself up by the aid of the oaken bar which formed the top of the stile. Having quoted a few lines of the Chinese poet Lo-tun-an to the effect that, however hard a knock might be, it might always conceivably be harder, I looked about for my coat, but could by no means find it.

"Henrietta," I said, "what have you done with my coat?"

"Look here, guv'nor," said the man from the dingle, "not so much Henrietta, if it's the same to you. This woman's my wife. Who are you to call her Henrietta?"

I assured the man from the dingle that I had meant no disrespect to his wife. "I had thought she was a mort," said I; "but the ria of a Romany chal is always sacred to me."

"Clean balmy," said the woman.

"Some other day," said I, "I may visit you in your camp in the dingle and read you the master's book about the Romanys."

"What's Romanys?" asked the man.

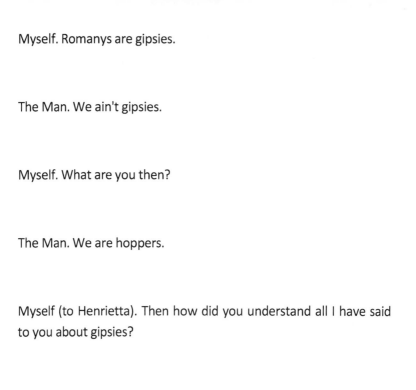

Myself. Romanys are gipsies.

The Man. We ain't gipsies.

Myself. What are you then?

The Man. We are hoppers.

Myself (to Henrietta). Then how did you understand all I have said to you about gipsies?

Henrietta. I didn't.

I again asked for my coat, but it was clear now that before offering to fight the florid-faced man with the mole over his left eyebrow I must have hung my coat upon the splashboard of his van. I therefore recited a verse from Ferideddin-Atar, the Persian poet, which signifies that it is more important to preserve your skin than your clothes, and bidding farewell to the man from the dingle and his wife I returned into the old English village of Swinehurst, where I was able to buy a second-hand coat, which enabled me to make my way to the station, where I should start for London. I could not but remark with some surprise that I was followed to the station by many of the villagers, together with the man with the shiny coat, and that other, the strange man, he who had slunk behind the clock-case. From time to time I turned and approached them, hoping to fall into conversation with them; but as I did so they would break and hasten down the road. Only the village constable came on, and he walked by my side and listened while I told him the history of Hunyadi Janos and the events which occurred during the wars between that hero, known also as Corvinus or the crow-like, and Mahommed the second, he who captured Constantinople, better known as Byzantium, before the Christian epoch. Together with the constable I entered the station, and seating myself in a carriage I took paper from my pocket and I began to write upon the paper all that had occurred to me, in order that I might show that it was not easy in these days to follow the example of the master. As I wrote, I heard the constable talk to the station-master, a stout, middle-sized man with a red neck-tie, and tell him of my own adventures in the old English village of Swinehurst.

"He is a gentleman too," said the constable, "and I doubt not that he lives in a big house in London town."

"A very big house if every man had his rights," said the station-master, and waving his hand he signalled that the train should proceed.

IV

THE MAN FROM ARCHANGEL

On the fourth day of March, in the year 1867, I being at that time in my five-and-twentieth year, I wrote down the following words in my note-book—the result of much mental perturbation and conflict:

"The solar system, amidst a countless number of other systems as large as itself, rolls ever silently through space in the direction of the constellation of Hercules. The great spheres of which it is composed spin and spin through the eternal void ceaselessly and noiselessly. Of these one of the smallest and most insignificant is that conglomeration of solid and of liquid particles which we have named the earth. It whirls onwards now as it has done before my birth, and will do after my death—a revolving mystery, coming none know whence, and going none know whither. Upon the outer crust of this moving mass crawl many mites, of whom I, John M'Vittie, am one, helpless, impotent, being dragged aimlessly through space. Yet such is the state of things amongst us that the little energy and glimmering of reason which I possess is entirely taken up with the labours which are necessary in order to procure certain metallic discs, wherewith I may purchase the chemical elements necessary to build up my ever-wasting tissues, and keep a roof over me to shelter me from the inclemency of the weather. I thus have no thought to expend upon the vital questions which surround me on every side. Yet, miserable entity as I am, I can still at times feel some degree of happiness, and am even—save the mark!—puffed up occasionally with a sense of my own importance."

These words, as I have said, I wrote down in my note-book, and they reflected accurately the thoughts which I found rooted far down in my soul, ever present and unaffected by the passing emotions of the hour. At last, however, came a time when my uncle, M'Vittie of Glencairn, died—the same who was at one time chairman of committees of the House of Commons. He divided his great wealth among his many nephews, and I found myself with sufficient to provide amply for my wants during the remainder of my life, and became at the same time the owner of a bleak tract of land upon the coast of Caithness, which I think the old man must have bestowed upon me in derision, for it was sandy and valueless, and he had ever a grim sense of humour. Up to this time I had been an attorney in a midland town in England. Now I saw that I could put my thoughts into effect, and, leaving all petty and sordid aims, could elevate my mind by the study of the secrets of nature. My departure from my English home was somewhat accelerated by the fact that I had nearly slain a man in a quarrel, for my temper was fiery, and I was apt to forget my own strength when enraged. There was no legal action taken in the matter, but the papers yelped at me, and folk looked askance when I met them. It ended by my cursing them and their vile, smoke-polluted town, and hurrying to my northern possession, where I might at last find peace and an opportunity for solitary study and contemplation. I borrowed from my capital before I went, and so was able to take with me a choice collection of the most modern philosophical instruments and books, together with chemicals and such other things as I might need in my retirement.

The land which I had inherited was a narrow strip, consisting mostly of sand, and extending for rather over two miles round the coast of Mansie Bay, in Caithness. Upon this strip there had been a rambling, grey-stone building—when erected or wherefore none could tell me—and this I had repaired, so that it made a dwelling quite good enough for one of my simple tastes. One room was my laboratory, another my sitting-room, and in a third, just under the sloping roof, I slung the hammock in which I always slept. There were three other rooms, but I left them vacant, except one which was given over to the old crone who kept house for me. Save the Youngs and the M'Leods, who were fisher-folk living round at the other side of Fergus Ness, there were no other people for many miles in each direction. In front of the house was the great bay, behind it were two long barren hills, capped by other loftier ones beyond. There was a glen between the hills, and when the wind was from the land it used to sweep down this with a melancholy sough and whisper among the branches of the fir-trees beneath my attic window.

I dislike my fellow-mortals. Justice compels me to add that they appear for the most part to dislike me. I hate their little crawling ways, their conventionalities, their deceits, their narrow rights and wrongs. They take offence at my brusque outspokenness, my disregard for their social laws, my impatience of all constraint. Among my books and my drugs in my lonely den at Mansie I could let the great drove of the human race pass onwards with their politics and inventions and tittle-tattle, and I remained behind stagnant and happy. Not stagnant either, for I was working in my own little groove, and making progress. I have reason to believe that Dalton's atomic theory is founded upon error, and I know that mercury is not an element.

During the day I was busy with my distillations and analyses. Often I forgot my meals, and when old Madge summoned me to my tea I found my dinner lying untouched upon the table. At night I read Bacon, Descartes, Spinoza, Kant—all those who have pried into what is unknowable. They are all fruitless and empty, barren of result, but prodigal of polysyllables, reminding me of men who, while digging for gold, have turned up many worms, and then exhibit then exultantly as being what they sought. At times a restless spirit would come upon me, and I would walk thirty and forty miles without rest or breaking fast. On those occasions, when I used to stalk through the country villages, gaunt, unshaven, and dishevelled, the mothers would rush into the road and drag their children indoors, and the rustics would swarm out of their pot-houses to gaze at me. I believe that I was known far and wide as the "mad laird o' Mansie." It was rarely, however, that I made these raids into the country, for I usually took my exercise upon my own beach, where I soothed my spirit with strong black tobacco, and made the ocean my friend and my confidant.

What companion is there like the great restless, throbbing sea? What human mood is there which it does not match and sympathise with? There are none so gay but that they may feel gayer when they listen to its merry turmoil, and see the long green surges racing in, with the glint of the sunbeams in their sparkling crests. But when the grey waves toss their heads in anger, and the wind screams above them, goading them on to madder and more tumultuous efforts, then the darkest-minded of men feels that there is a melancholy principle in Nature which is as gloomy as his own thoughts. When it was calm in the Bay of Mansie the surface would be as clear and bright as a sheet of silver, broken only at one spot some little way from the shore, where a long black line projected out of the water looking like the jagged back of some sleeping monster. This was the top of the dangerous ridge of rocks known to the fishermen as the "ragged reef o' Mansie." When the wind blew from the east the waves would break upon it like thunder, and the spray would be tossed far over my house and up to the hills behind. The bay itself was a bold and noble one, but too much exposed to the northern and eastern gales, and too much dreaded for its reef, to be much used by mariners. There was something of romance about this lonely spot. I have lain in my boat upon a calm day, and peering over the edge I have seen far down the flickering, ghostly forms of great fish—fish, as it seemed to me, such as naturalist never knew, and which my imagination transformed into the genii of that desolate bay. Once, as I stood by the brink of the waters upon a quiet night, a great cry, as of a woman in hopeless grief, rose from the bosom of the deep, and swelled out upon the still air, now sinking and now rising, for a space of thirty seconds. This I heard with my own ears.

In this strange spot, with the eternal hills behind me and the eternal sea in front, I worked and brooded for more than two years unpestered by my fellow men. By degrees I had trained my old servant into habits of silence, so that she now rarely opened her lips, though I doubt not that when twice a year she visited her relations in Wick, her tongue during those few days made up for its enforced rest. I had come almost to forget that I was a member of the human family, and to live entirely with the dead whose books I pored over, when a sudden incident occurred which threw all my thoughts into a new channel.

Three rough days in June had been succeeded by one calm and peaceful one. There was not a breath of air that evening. The sun sank down in the west behind a line of purple clouds, and the smooth surface of the bay was gashed with scarlet streaks. Along the beach the pools left by the tide showed up like gouts of blood against the yellow sand, as if some wounded giant had toilfully passed that way, and had left these red traces of his grievous hurt behind him. As the darkness closed in, certain ragged clouds which had lain low on the eastern horizon coalesced and formed a great irregular cumulus. The glass was still low, and I knew that there was mischief brewing. About nine o'clock a dull moaning sound came up from the sea, as from a creature, who, much harassed, learns that the hour of suffering has come round again. At ten a sharp breeze sprang up from the eastward. At eleven it had increased to a gale, and by midnight the most furious storm was raging which I ever remember upon that weather-beaten coast.

As I went to bed the shingle and seaweed were pattering up against my attic window, and the wind was screaming as though every gust were a lost soul. By that time the sounds of the tempest had become a lullaby to me. I knew that the grey walls of the old house would buffet it out, and for what occurred in the world outside I had small concern. Old Madge was usually as callous to such things as I was myself. It was a surprise to me when, about three in the morning, I was awoke by the sound of a great knocking at my door and excited cries in the wheezy voice of my housekeeper. I sprang out of my hammock, and roughly demanded of her what was the matter.

"Eh, maister, maister!" she screamed in her hateful dialect. "Come doun, mun; come doun! There's a muckle ship gaun ashore on the reef, and the puir folks are a' yammerin' and ca'in' for help—and I doobt they'll a' be drooned. Oh, Maister M'Vittie, come doun!"

"Hold your tongue, you hag!" I shouted back in a passion. "What is it to you whether they are drowned or not? Get back to your bed and leave me alone." I turned in again and drew the blankets over me. "Those men out there," I said to myself, "have already gone through half the horrors of death. If they be saved they will but have to go through the same once more in the space of a few brief years. It is best therefore that they should pass away now, since they have suffered that anticipation which is more than the pain of dissolution." With this thought in my mind I endeavoured to compose myself to sleep once more, for that philosophy which had taught me to consider death as a small and trivial incident in man's eternal and ever-changing career, had also broken me of much curiosity concerning worldly matters. On this occasion I found, however, that the old leaven still fermented strongly in my soul. I tossed from side to side for some minutes endeavouring to beat down the impulses of the moment by the rules of conduct which I had framed during months of thought. Then I heard a dull roar amid the wild shriek of the gale, and I knew that it was the sound of a signal-gun. Driven by an uncontrollable impulse, I rose, dressed, and having lit my pipe, walked out on to the beach.

It was pitch dark when I came outside, and the wind blew with such violence that I had to put my shoulder against it and push my way along the shingle. My face pringled and smarted with the sting of the gravel which was blown against it, and the red ashes of my pipe streamed away behind me, dancing fantastically through the darkness. I went down to where the great waves were thundering in, and shading my eyes with my hands to keep off the salt spray, I peered out to sea. I could distinguish nothing, and yet it seemed to me that shouts and great inarticulate cries were borne to me by the blasts. Suddenly as I gazed I made out the glint of a light, and then the whole bay and the beach were lit up in a moment by a vivid blue glare. They were burning a coloured signal-light on board of the vessel. There she lay on her beam ends right in the centre of the jagged reef, hurled over to such an angle that I could see all the planking of her deck. She was a large two-masted schooner, of foreign rig, and lay perhaps a hundred and eighty or two hundred yards from the shore. Every spar and rope and writhing piece of cordage showed up hard and clear under the livid light which sputtered and flickered from the highest portion of the forecastle. Beyond the doomed ship out of the great darkness came the long rolling lines of black waves, never ending, never tiring, with a petulant tuft of foam here and there upon their crests. Each as it reached the broad circle of unnatural light appeared to gather strength and volume, and to hurry on more impetuously until, with a roar and a jarring crash, it sprang upon its victim. Clinging to the weather shrouds I could distinctly see some ten or twelve frightened seamen, who, when their light revealed my presence, turned their white faces towards me and waved their hands imploringly. I felt my gorge rise against these poor cowering worms. Why should they presume to shirk the narrow pathway along which all that is great and noble among mankind has travelled? There was one there who interested me more than they. He was a tall man, who stood apart from the others, balancing himself upon the swaying wreck as though he disdained to cling to rope or bulwark. His hands were clasped behind his back and his head was sunk upon his breast, but even in that despondent attitude there was a litheness and decision in his pose and in every motion which marked him as a man little likely to yield to despair. Indeed, I could see by his occasional rapid glances up and down and all around him that he was weighing every chance of safety, but though he often gazed across the raging surf to where he could see my dark figure upon the beach, his self-respect or some other reason forbade him from imploring my help in any way. He stood, dark, silent, and inscrutable, looking down on the black sea, and waiting for whatever fortune Fate might send him.

It seemed to me that that problem would very soon be settled. As I looked, an enormous billow, topping all the others, and coming after them, like a driver following a flock, swept over the vessel. Her foremast snapped short off, and the men who clung to the shrouds were brushed away like a swarm of flies. With a rending, riving sound the ship began to split in two, where the sharp back of the Mansie reef was sawing into her keel. The solitary man upon the forecastle ran rapidly across the deck and seized hold of a white bundle which I had already observed but failed to make out. As he lifted it up the light fell upon it, and I saw that the object was a woman, with a spar lashed across her body and under her arms in such a way that her head should always rise above water. He bore her tenderly to the side and seemed to speak for a minute or so to her, as though explaining the impossibility of remaining upon the ship. Her answer was a singular one. I saw her deliberately raise her hand and strike him across the face with it. He appeared to be silenced for a moment or so by this, but he addressed her again, directing her, as far as I could gather from his motions, how she should behave when in the water. She shrank away from him, but he caught her in his arms. He stooped over her for a moment and seemed to press his lips against her forehead. Then a great wave came welling up against the side of the breaking vessel, and leaning over he placed her upon the summit of it as gently as a child might be committed to its cradle. I saw her white dress flickering among the foam on the crest of the dark billow, and then the light sank gradually lower, and the riven ship and its lonely occupant were hidden from my eyes.

As I watched those things my manhood overcame my philosophy, and I felt a frantic impulse to be up and doing. I threw my cynicism to one side as a garment which I might don again at leisure, and I rushed wildly to my boat and my sculls. She was a leaky tub, but what then? Was I, who had cast many a wistful, doubtful glance at my opium bottle, to begin now to weigh chances and to cavil at danger? I dragged her down to the sea with the strength of a maniac and sprang in. For a moment or two it was a question whether she could live among the boiling surge, but a dozen frantic strokes took me through it, half full of water but still afloat. I was out on the unbroken waves now, at one time climbing, climbing up the broad black breast of one, then sinking down, down on the other side, until looking up I could see the gleam of the foam all around me against the dark heavens. Far behind me I could hear the wild wailings of old Madge, who, seeing me start, thought no doubt that my madness had come to a climax. As I rowed I peered over my shoulder, until at last on the belly of a great wave which was sweeping towards me I distinguished the vague white outline of the woman. Stooping over, I seized her as she swept by me, and with an effort lifted her, all sodden with water, into the boat. There was no need to row back, for the next billow carried us in and threw us upon the beach. I dragged the boat out of danger, and then lifting up the woman I carried her to the house, followed by my housekeeper, loud with congratulation and praise.

Now that I had done this thing a reaction set in upon me. I felt that my burden lived, for I heard the faint beat of her heart as I pressed my ear against her side in carrying her. Knowing this, I threw her down beside the fire which Madge had lit, with as little sympathy as though she had been a bundle of fagots. I never glanced at her to see if she were fair or no. For many years I had cared little for the face of a woman. As I lay in my hammock upstairs, however, I heard the old woman as she chafed the warmth back into her, crooning a chorus of, "Eh, the puir lassie! Eh, the bonnie lassie!" from which I gathered that this piece of jetsam was both young and comely.

The morning after the gale was peaceful and sunny. As I walked along the long sweep of sand I could hear the panting of the sea. It was heaving and swirling about the reef, but along the shore it rippled in gently enough. There was no sign of the schooner, nor was there any wreckage upon the beach, which did not surprise me, as I knew there was a great undertow in those waters. A couple of broad-winged gulls were hovering and skimming over the scene of the shipwreck, as though many strange things were visible to them beneath the waves. At times I could hear their raucous voices as they spoke to one another of what they saw.

When I came back from my walk the woman was waiting at the door for me. I began to wish when I saw her that I had never saved her, for here was an end of my privacy. She was very young—at the most nineteen, with a pale somewhat refined face, yellow hair, merry blue eyes, and shining teeth. Her beauty was of an ethereal type. She looked so white and light and fragile that she might have been the spirit of that storm-foam from out of which I plucked her. She had wreathed some of Madge's garments round her in a way which was quaint and not unbecoming. As I strode heavily up the pathway, she put out her hands with a pretty, child-like gesture, and ran down towards me, meaning, as I surmise, to thank me for having saved her, but I put her aside with a wave of my hand and passed her. At this she seemed somewhat hurt, and the tears sprang into her eyes, but she followed me into the sitting room and watched me wistfully. "What country do you come from?" I asked her suddenly.

She smiled when I spoke, but shook her head.

"Français?" I asked. "Deutsch?" "Espagnol?"—each time she shook her head, and then she rippled off into a long statement in some tongue of which I could not understand one word.

After breakfast was over, however, I got a clue to her nationality. Passing along the beach once more, I saw that in a cleft of the ridge a piece of wood had been jammed. I rowed out to it in my boat, and brought it ashore. It was part of the sternpost of a boat, and on it, or rather on the piece of wood attached to it, was the word

"Archangel," painted in strange, quaint lettering. "So," I thought, as I paddled slowly back, "this pale damsel is a Russian. A fit subject for the White Czar and a proper dweller on the shores of the White Sea!" It seemed to me strange that one of her apparent refinement should perform so long a journey in so frail a craft. When I came back into the house, I pronounced the word "Archangel" several times in different intonations, but she did not appear to recognise it.

I shut myself up in the laboratory all the morning, continuing a research which I was making upon the nature of the allotropic forms of carbon and of sulphur. When I came out at mid-day for some food she was sitting, by the table with a needle and thread, mending some rents in her clothes, which were now dry. I resented her continued presence, but I could not turn her out on the beach to shift for herself. Presently she presented a new phase of her character. Pointing to herself and then to the scene of the shipwreck, she held up one finger, by which I understood her to be asking whether she was the only one saved. I nodded my head to indicate that she was. On this she sprang out of her chair with a cry of great joy, and holding the garment which she was mending over her head, and swaying it from side to side with the motion of her body, she danced as lightly as a feather all round the room, and then out through the open door into the sunshine. As she whirled round she sang in a plaintive shrill voice some uncouth barbarous chant, expressive of exultation. I called out to her, "Come in, you young fiend, come in and be silent!" but she went on with her dance. Then she suddenly ran towards me, and catching my hand before I could pluck it away, she kissed it. While we were at dinner she spied one of my pencils, and taking it up she wrote the two words "Sophie Ramusine" upon a piece of paper, and then pointed to herself as a sign that that was her name. She handed the pencil to me, evidently expecting that I would be equally communicative, but I put it in my pocket as a sign that I wished to hold no intercourse with her.

Every moment of my life now I regretted the unguarded precipitancy with which I had saved this woman. What was it to me whether she had lived or died? I was no young, hot-headed youth to do such things. It was bad enough to be compelled to have Madge in the house, but she was old and ugly, and could be ignored. This one was young and lively, and so fashioned as to divert attention from graver things. Where could I send her, and what could I do with her? If I sent information to Wick it would mean that officials and others would come to me and pry, and peep, and chatter—a hateful thought. It was better to endure her presence than that.

I soon found that there were fresh troubles in store for me. There is no place safe from the swarming, restless race of which I am a member. In the evening, when the sun was dipping down behind the hills, casting them into dark shadow, but gilding the sands and casting a great glory over the sea, I went, as is my custom, for a stroll along the beach. Sometimes on these occasions I took my book with me. I did so on this night, and stretching myself upon a sand-dune I composed myself to read. As I lay there I suddenly became aware of a shadow which interposed itself between the sun and myself. Looking round, I saw to my great surprise a very tall, powerful man, who was standing a few yards off, and who, instead of looking at me, was ignoring my existence completely, and was gazing over my head with a stern set face at the bay and the black line of the Mansie reef. His complexion was dark, with black hair, and short, curling beard, a hawk-like nose, and golden earrings in his ears—the general effect being wild and somewhat noble. He wore a faded velveteen jacket, a red-flannel shirt, and high sea boots, coming half-way up his thighs. I recognised him at a glance as being the same man who had been left on the wreck the night before.

"Hullo!" I said, in an aggrieved voice. "You got ashore all right, then?"

"Yes," he answered, in good English. "It was no doing of mine. The waves threw me up. I wish to God I had been allowed to drown!" There was a slight foreign lisp in his accent which was rather pleasing. "Two good fishermen, who live round yonder point, pulled me out and cared for me; yet I could not honestly thank them for it."

"Ho! ho!" thought I, "here is a man of my own kidney."

"Why do you wish to be drowned?" I asked.

"Because," he cried, throwing out his long arms with a passionate, despairing gesture, "there—there in that blue smiling bay, lies my soul, my treasure—everything that I loved and lived for."

"Well, well," I said. "People are ruined every day, but there's no use making a fuss about it. Let me inform you that this ground on which you walk is my ground, and that the sooner you take yourself off it the better pleased I shall be. One of you is quite trouble enough."

"One of us?" he gasped.

"Yes—if you could take her off with you I should be still more grateful."

He gazed at me for a moment as if hardly able to realise what I said, and then with a wild cry he ran away from me with prodigious speed and raced along the sands towards my house. Never before or since have I seen a human being run so fast. I followed as rapidly as I could, furious at this threatened invasion, but long before I reached the house he had disappeared through the open door. I heard a great scream from the inside, and as I came nearer the sound of a man's bass voice speaking rapidly and loudly. When I looked in, the girl, Sophie Ramusine, was crouching in a corner, cowering away, with fear and loathing expressed on her averted face and in every line of her shrinking form. The other, with his dark eyes flashing, and his outstretched hands quivering with emotion, was pouring forth a torrent of passionate pleading words. He made a step forward to her as I entered, but she writhed still further away, and uttered a sharp cry like that of a rabbit when the weasel has him by the throat.

"Here!" I said, pulling him back from her. "This is a pretty to-do! What do you mean? Do you think this is a wayside inn or place of public accommodation?"

"Oh, sir," he said, "excuse me. This woman is my wife, and I feared that she was drowned. You have brought me back to life."

"Who are you?" I asked roughly.

"I am a man from Archangel," he said simply; "a Russian man."

"What is your name?"

"Ourganeff."

"Ourganeff!—and hers is Sophie Ramusine. She is no wife of yours. She has no ring."

"We are man and wife in the sight of Heaven," he said solemnly, looking upwards. "We are bound by higher laws than those of earth." As he spoke the girl slipped behind me and caught me by the other hand, pressing it as though beseeching my protection.

"Give me up my wife, sir," he went on. "Let me take her away from here."

"Look here, you—whatever your name is," I said sternly; "I don't want this wench here. I wish I had never seen her. If she died it would be no grief to me. But as to handing her over to you, when it is clear she fears and hates you, I won't do it. So now just clear your great body out of this, and leave me to my books. I hope I may never look upon your face again."

"You won't give her up to me?" he said hoarsely.

"I'll see you damned first!" I answered.

"Suppose I take her," he cried, his dark face growing darker.

All my tigerish blood flashed up in a moment. I picked up a billet of wood from beside the fireplace. "Go," I said, in a low voice, "go quick, or I may do you an injury." He looked at me irresolutely for a moment, and then he left the house. He came back again in a moment, however, and stood in the doorway looking in at us.

"Have a heed what you do," he said. "The woman is mine, and I shall have her. When it comes to blows, a Russian is as good a man as a Scotchman."

"We shall see that," I cried, springing forward, but he was already gone, and I could see his tall form moving away through the gathering darkness.

For a month or more after this things went smoothly with us. I never spoke to the Russian girl, nor did she ever address me. Sometimes when I was at work in my laboratory she would slip inside the door and sit silently there watching me with her great eyes. At first this intrusion annoyed me, but by degrees, finding that she made no attempt to distract my attention, I suffered her to remain. Encouraged by this concession, she gradually came to move the stool on which she sat nearer and nearer to my table, until after gaining a little every day during some weeks, she at last worked her way right up to me, and used to perch herself beside me whenever I worked. In this position she used, still without ever obtruding her presence in any way, to make herself very useful by holding my pens, test-tubes, or bottles and handing me whatever I wanted, with never-failing sagacity. By ignoring the fact of her being a human being, and looking upon her as a useful automatic machine, I accustomed myself to her presence so far as to miss her on the few occasions when she was not at her post. I have a habit of talking aloud to myself at times when I work, so as to fix my results better in my mind. The girl must have had a surprising memory for sounds, for she could always repeat the words which I let fall in this way, without, of course, understanding in the least what they meant. I have often been amused at hearing her discharge a volley of chemical equations and algebraic symbols at old Madge, and then burst into a ringing laugh when the crone would shake her head, under the impression, no doubt, that she was being addressed in Russian.

She never went more than a few yards from the house, and indeed never put her foot over the threshold without looking carefully out of each window in order to be sure that there was nobody about. By this I knew that she suspected that her fellow-countryman was still in the neighbourhood, and feared that he might attempt to carry her off. She did something else which was significant. I had an old revolver with some cartridges, which had been thrown away among the rubbish. She found this one day, and at once proceeded to clean it and oil it. She hung it up near the door, with the cartridges in a little bag beside it, and whenever I went for a walk, she would take it down and insist upon my carrying it with me. In my absence she would always bolt the door. Apart from her apprehensions she seemed fairly happy, busying herself in helping Madge when she was not attending upon me. She was wonderfully nimble-fingered and natty in all domestic duties.

It was not long before I discovered that her suspicions were well founded, and that this man from Archangel was still lurking in the vicinity. Being restless one night I rose and peered out of the window. The weather was somewhat cloudy, and I could barely make out the line of the sea, and the loom of my boat upon the beach. As I gazed, however, and my eyes became accustomed to the obscurity, I became aware that there was some other dark blur upon the sands, and that in front of my very door, where certainly there had been nothing of the sort the preceding night. As I stood at my diamond-paned lattice, still peering and peeping to make out what this might be, a great bank of clouds rolled slowly away from the face of the moon, and a flood of cold, clear light was poured down upon the silent bay and the long sweep of its desolate shores. Then I saw what this was which haunted my doorstep. It was he, the Russian. He squatted there like a gigantic toad, with his legs doubled under him in strange Mongolian fashion, and his eyes fixed apparently upon the window of the room in which the young girl and the housekeeper slept. The light fell upon his upturned face, and I saw once more the hawk-like grace of his countenance, with the single deeply-indented line of care upon his brow, and the protruding beard which marks the passionate nature. My first impulse was to shoot him as a trespasser, but, as I gazed, my resentment changed into pity and contempt "Poor fool," I said to myself, "is it then possible that you, whom I have seen looking open-eyed at present death, should have your whole thoughts and ambitions centred upon this wretched slip of a girl—a girl, too, who flies from you and hates you? Most women would love you—were it but for that dark face and great handsome body of yours—and yet you must needs hanker after the one in a thousand who will have no traffic with you." As I returned to my bed I chuckled much to myself over this thought. I knew that my bars were strong and my bolts thick. It mattered little to me whether this strange man spent his night at my door or a hundred leagues off, so long as he was gone by the morning. As I expected, when I rose and went out, there was no sign of him, nor had he left any trace of his midnight vigil.

It was not long, however, before I saw him again. I had been out for a row one morning, for my head was aching, partly from prolonged stooping, and partly from the effects of a noxious drug which I had inhaled the night before. I pulled along the coast some miles, and then, feeling thirsty, I landed at a place where I knew that a fresh water stream trickled down into the sea. This rivulet passed through my land, but the mouth of it, where I found myself that day, was beyond my boundary line. I felt somewhat taken aback when rising from the stream at which I had slaked my thirst I found myself face to face with the Russian. I was as much a trespasser now as he was, and I could see at a glance that he knew it.

"I wish to speak a few words to you," he said gravely.

"Hurry up, then!" I answered, glancing at my watch. "I have no time to listen to chatter."

"Chatter!" he repeated angrily. "Ah, but there. You Scotch people are strange men. Your face is hard and your words rough, but so are those of the good fishermen with whom I stay, yet I find that beneath it all there lie kind honest natures. No doubt you are kind and good, too, in spite of your roughness."

"In the name of the devil," I said, "say your say, and go your way. I am weary of the sight of you."

"Can I not soften you in any way?" he cried. "Ah, see—see here"— he produced a small Grecian cross from inside his velvet jacket.

"Look at this. Our religions may differ in form, but at least we have some common thoughts and feelings when we see this emblem."

"I am not so sure of that," I answered.

He looked at me thoughtfully.

"You are a very strange man," he said at last. "I cannot understand you. You still stand between me and Sophie. It is a dangerous position to take, sir. Oh, believe me, before it is too late. If you did but know what I have done to gain that woman—how I have risked my body, how I have lost my soul! You are a small obstacle to some which I have surmounted—you, whom a rip with a knife, or a blow from a stone, would put out of my way for ever. But God preserve me from that," he cried wildly. "I am deep—too deep—already. Anything rather than that."

"You would do better to go back to your country," I said, "than to skulk about these sand-hills and disturb my leisure. When I have proof that you have gone away I shall hand this woman over to the protection of the Russian Consul at Edinburgh. Until then, I shall guard her myself, and not you, nor any Muscovite that ever breathed, shall take her from me."

"And what is your object in keeping me from Sophie?" he asked. "Do you imagine that I would injure her? Why man, I would give my life freely to save her from the slightest harm. Why do you do this thing?"

"I do it because it is my good pleasure to act so," I answered. "I give no man reasons for my conduct."

"Look here!" he cried, suddenly blazing into fury, and advancing towards me with his shaggy mane bristling and his brown hands clenched. "If I thought you had one dishonest thought towards this girl—if for a moment I had reason to believe that you had any base motive for detaining her—as sure as there is a God in Heaven I should drag the heart out of your bosom with my hands." The very idea seemed to have put the man in a frenzy, for his face was all distorted and his hands opened and shut convulsively. I thought that he was about to spring at my throat.

"Stand off," I said, putting my hand on my pistol. "If you lay a finger on me I shall kill you."

He put his hand into his pocket, and for a moment I thought he was about to produce a weapon too, but instead of that he whipped out a cigarette and lit it, breathing the smoke rapidly into his lungs. No doubt he had found by experience that this was the most effectual way of curbing his passions.

"I told you," he said in a quieter voice, "that my name is Ourganeff—Alexis Ourganeff. I am a Finn by birth, but I have spent my life in every part of the world. I was one who could never be still, nor settle down to a quiet existence. After I came to own my own ship there is hardly a port from Archangel to Australia which I have not entered. I was rough and wild and free, but there was one at home, sir, who was prim and white-handed and soft-tongued, skilful in little fancies and conceits which women love. This youth by his wiles and tricks stole from me the love of the girl whom I had ever marked as my own, and who up to that time had seemed in some sort inclined to return my passion. I had been on a voyage to Hammerfest for ivory, and coming back unexpectedly I learned that my pride and treasure was to be married to this soft-skinned boy, and that the party had actually gone to the church. In such moments, sir, something gives way in my head, and I hardly know what I do. I landed with a boat's crew—all men who had sailed with me for years, and who were as true as steel. We went up to the church. They were standing, she and he, before the priest, but the thing had not been done. I dashed between them and caught her round the waist. My men beat back the frightened bridegroom and the lookers on. We bore her down to the boat and aboard our vessel, and then getting up anchor we sailed away across the White Sea until the spires of Archangel sank down behind the horizon. She had my cabin, my room, every comfort. I slept among the men in the forecastle. I hoped that in time her aversion to me would wear away, and that she would consent to marry me in England or in France. For days and days we sailed. We saw the North Cape die away behind us, and we skirted the grey Norwegian coast, but still, in spite of every attention, she would not forgive me for tearing her from that pale-faced lover of hers. Then came this cursed storm which shattered both my ship and my hopes, and has deprived me even of the sight of the woman for whom I have risked so much.

Perhaps she may learn to love me yet. You, sir," he said wistfully, "look like one who has seen much of the world. Do you not think that she may come to forget this man and to love me?"

"I am tired of your story," I said, turning away. "For my part, I think you are a great fool. If you imagine that this love of yours will pass away you had best amuse yourself as best you can until it does. If, on the other hand, it is a fixed thing, you cannot do better than cut your throat, for that is the shortest way out of it. I have no more time to waste on the matter." With this I hurried away and walked down to the boat. I never looked round, but I heard the dull sound of his feet upon the sands as he followed me.

"I have told you the beginning of my story," he said, "and you shall know the end some day. You would do well to let the girl go."

I never answered him, but pushed the boat off. When I had rowed some distance out I looked back and saw his tall figure upon the yellow sand as he stood gazing thoughtfully after me. When I looked again some minutes later he had disappeared.

For a long time after this my life was as regular and as monotonous as it had been before the shipwreck. At times I hoped that the man from Archangel had gone away altogether, but certain footsteps which I saw upon the sand, and more particularly a little pile of cigarette ash which I found one day behind a hillock from which a view of the house might be obtained, warned me that, though invisible, he was still in the vicinity. My relations with the Russian girl remained the same as before. Old Madge had been somewhat jealous of her presence at first, and seemed to fear that what little authority she had would be taken away from her. By degrees, however, as she came to realise my utter indifference, she became reconciled to the situation, and, as I have said before, profited by it, as our visitor performed much of the domestic work.

And now I am coming near the end of this narrative of mine, which I have written a great deal more for my own amusement than for that of any one else. The termination of the strange episode in which these two Russians had played a part was as wild and as sudden as the commencement. The events of one single night freed me from all my troubles, and left me once more alone with my books and my studies, as I had been before their intrusion. Let me endeavour to describe how this came about.

I had had a long day of heavy and wearying work, so that in the evening I determined upon taking a long walk. When I emerged from the house my attention was attracted by the appearance of the sea. It lay like a sheet of glass, so that never a ripple disturbed its surface. Yet the air was filled with that indescribable moaning sound which I have alluded to before—a sound as though the spirits of all those who lay beneath those treacherous waters were sending a sad warning of coming troubles to their brethren in the flesh. The fishermen's wives along that coast know the eerie sound, and look anxiously across the waters for the brown sails making for the land. When I heard it I stepped back into the house and looked at the glass. It was down below 29°. Then I knew that a wild night was coming upon us.

Underneath the hills where I walked that evening it was dull and chill, but their summits were rosy-red, and the sea was brightened by the sinking sun. There were no clouds of importance in the sky, yet the dull groaning of the sea grew louder and stronger. I saw, far to the eastward, a brig beating up for Wick, with a reef in her topsails. It was evident that her captain had read the signs of nature as I had done. Behind her a long, lurid haze lay low upon the water, concealing the horizon. "I had better push on," I thought to myself, "or the wind may rise before I can get back."

I suppose I must have been at least half a mile from the house when I suddenly stopped and listened breathlessly. My ears were so accustomed to the noises of nature, the sighing of the breeze and the sob of the waves, that any other sound made itself heard at a great distance. I waited, listening with all my ears. Yes, there it was again—a long-drawn, shrill cry of despair, ringing over the sands and echoed back from the hills behind me—a piteous appeal for aid. It came from the direction of my house. I turned and ran back homewards at the top of my speed, ploughing through the sand, racing over the shingle. In my mind there was a great dim perception of what had occurred.

About a quarter of a mile from the house there is a high sand-hill, from which the whole country round is visible. When I reached the top of this I paused for a moment. There was the old grey building—there the boat. Everything seemed to be as I had left it. Even as I gazed, however, the shrill scream was repeated, louder than before, and the next moment a tall figure emerged from my door, the figure of the Russian sailor. Over his shoulder was the white form of the young girl, and even in his haste he seemed to bear her tenderly and with gentle reverence. I could hear her wild cries and see her desperate struggles to break away from him. Behind the couple came my old housekeeper, staunch and true, as the aged dog, who can no longer bite, still snarls with toothless gums at the intruder. She staggered feebly along at the heels of the ravisher, waving her long, thin arms, and hurling, no doubt, volleys of Scotch curses and imprecations at his head. I saw at a glance that he was making for the boat. A sudden hope sprang up in my soul that I might be in time to intercept him. I ran for the beach at the top of my speed. As I ran I slipped a cartridge into my revolver. This I determined should be the last of these invasions.

I was too late. By the time I reached the water's edge he was a hundred yards away, making the boat spring with every stroke of his powerful arms. I uttered a wild cry of impotent anger, and stamped up and down the sands like a maniac. He turned and saw me. Rising from his seat he made me a graceful bow, and waved his hand to me. It was not a triumphant or a derisive gesture. Even my furious and distempered mind recognised it as being a solemn and courteous leave-taking. Then he settled down to his oars once more, and the little skiff shot away out over the bay. The sun had gone down now, leaving a single dull, red streak upon the water, which stretched away until it blended with the purple haze on the horizon. Gradually the skiff grew smaller and smaller as it sped across this lurid band, until the shades of night gathered round it and it became a mere blur upon the lonely sea. Then this vague loom died away also and darkness settled over it—a darkness which should never be raised.

And why did I pace the solitary shore, hot and wrathful as a wolf whose whelp has been torn from it? Was it that I loved this Muscovite girl? No—a thousand times no. I am not one who, for the sake of a white skin or a blue eye, would belie my own life, and change the whole tenor of my thoughts and existence. My heart was untouched. But my pride—ah, there I had been cruelly wounded. To think that I had been unable to afford protection to the helpless one who craved it of me, and who relied on me! It was that which made my heart sick and sent the blood buzzing through my ears.

That night a great wind rose up from the sea, and the wild waves shrieked upon the shore as though they would tear it back with them into the ocean. The turmoil and the uproar were congenial to my vexed spirit. All night I wandered up and down, wet with spray and rain, watching the gleam of the white breakers and listening to the outcry of the storm. My heart was bitter against the Russian. I joined my feeble pipe to the screaming of the gale. "If he would but come back again!" I cried, with clenched hands; "if he would but come back!"

He came back. When the grey light of morning spread over the eastern sky, and lit up the great waste of yellow, tossing waters, with the brown clouds drifting swiftly over them, then I saw him once again. A few hundred yards off along the sand there lay a long dark object, cast up by the fury of the waves. It was my boat, much shattered and splintered. A little farther on, a vague, shapeless something was washing to and fro in the shallow water, all mixed with shingle and with seaweed. I saw at a glance that it was the Russian, face downwards and dead. I rushed into the water and dragged him up on to the beach. It was only when I turned him over that I discovered that she was beneath him, his dead arms encircling her, his mangled body still intervening between her and the fury of the storm. It seemed that the fierce German Sea might beat the life from him, but with all its strength it was unable to tear this one-idea'd man from the woman whom he loved. There were signs which led me to believe that during that awful night the woman's fickle mind had come at last to learn the worth of the true heart and strong arm which struggled for her and guarded her so tenderly. Why else should her little head be nestling so lovingly on his broad breast, while her yellow hair entwined itself with his flowing beard? Why too should there be that bright smile of ineffable happiness and triumph, which death itself had not had power to banish from his dusky face? I fancy that death had been brighter to him than life had ever been.

Madge and I buried them there on the shores of the desolate northern sea. They lie in one grave deep down beneath the yellow sand. Strange things may happen in the world around them. Empires may rise and may fall, dynasties may perish, great wars may come and go, but, heedless of it all, those two shall embrace each other for ever and aye, in their lonely shrine by the side of the sounding ocean. I sometimes have thought that their spirits flit like shadowy sea-mews over the wild waters of the bay. No cross or symbol marks their resting-place, but old Madge puts wild flowers upon it at times, and when I pass on my daily walk and see the fresh blossoms scattered over the sand, I think of the strange couple who came from afar, and broke for a little space the dull tenor of my sombre life.

V

THE GREAT BROWN-PERICORD MOTOR

It was a cold, foggy, dreary evening in May. Along the Strand blurred patches of light marked the position of the lamps. The flaring shop windows flickered vaguely with steamy brightness through the thick and heavy atmosphere.

The high lines of houses which led down to the Embankment were all dark and deserted, or illuminated only by the glimmering lamp of the caretaker. At one point, however, there shone out from three windows upon the second floor a rich flood of light, which broke the sombre monotony of the terrace. Passers-by glanced up curiously, and drew each others' attention to the ruddy glare, for it marked the chambers of Francis Pericord, the inventor and electrical engineer. Long into the watches of the night the gleam of his lamps bore witness to the untiring energy and restless industry which was rapidly carrying him to the first rank in his profession.

Within the chamber sat two men. The one was Pericord himself— hawk-faced and angular, with the black hair and brisk bearing which spoke of his Celtic origin. The other—thick, sturdy, and blue-eyed, was Jeremy Brown, the well-known mechanician. They had been partners in many an invention, in which the creative genius of the one had been aided by the practical abilities of the other. It was a question among their friends as to which was the better man.

It was no chance visit which had brought Brown into Pericord's workshop at so late an hour. Business was to be done—business which was to decide the failure or success of months of work, and which might affect their whole careers. Between them lay a long brown table, stained and corroded by strong acids, and littered with giant carboys, Faure's accumulators, voltaic piles, coils of wire, and great blocks of nonconducting porcelain. In the midst of all this lumber there stood a singular whizzing, whirring machine, upon which the eyes of both partners were riveted.

A small square metal receptacle was connected by numerous wires to a broad steel girdle, furnished on either side with two powerful projecting joints. The girdle was motionless, but the joints with the short arms attached to them flashed round every few seconds, with a pause between each rhythmic turn. The power which moved them came evidently from the metal box. A subtle odour of ozone was in the air.

"How about the flanges, Brown?" asked the inventor.

"They were too large to bring. They are seven foot by three. There is power enough there to work them however. I will answer for that."

"Aluminium with an alloy of copper?"

"Yes."

"See how beautifully it works." Pericord stretched out a thin, nervous hand, and pressed a button upon the machine. The joints revolved more slowly, and came presently to a dead stop. Again he touched a spring and the arms shivered and woke up again into their crisp metallic life. "The experimenter need not exert his muscular powers," he remarked. "He has only to be passive, and use his intelligence."

"Thanks to my motor," said Brown.

"Our motor," the other broke in sharply.

"Oh, of course," said his colleague impatiently. "The motor which you thought of, and which I reduced to practice—call it what you like."

"I call it the Brown-Pericord Motor," cried the inventor, with an angry flash of his dark eyes. "You worked out the details, but the abstract thought is mine, and mine alone."

"An abstract thought won't turn an engine," said Brown doggedly.

"That was why I took you into partnership," the other retorted, drumming nervously with his fingers upon the table. "I invent, you build. It is a fair division of labour."

Brown pursed up his lips, as though by no means satisfied upon the point. Seeing, however, that further argument was useless, he turned his attention to the machine, which was shivering and rocking with each swing of its arms, as though a very little more would send it skimming from the table.

"Is it not splendid?" cried Pericord.

"It is satisfactory," said the more phlegmatic Anglo-Saxon.

"There's immortality in it!"

"There's money in it!"

"Our names will go down with Montgolfier's."

"With Rothschild's, I hope."

"No, no, Brown; you take too material a view," cried the inventor, raising his gleaming eyes from the machine to his companion. "Our fortunes are a mere detail. Money is a thing which every heavy-witted plutocrat in the country shares with us. My hopes rise to something higher than that. Our true reward will come in the gratitude and goodwill of the human race."

Brown shrugged his shoulders. "You may have my share of that," he said. "I am a practical man. We must test our invention."

"Where can we do it?"

"That is what I wanted to speak about. It must be absolutely secret. If we had private grounds of our own it would be an easy matter, but there is no privacy in London."

"We must take it into the country."

"I have a suggestion to offer," said Brown. "My brother has a place in Sussex on the high land near Beachy Head. There is, I remember, a large and lofty barn near the house. Will is in Scotland, but the key is always at my disposal. Why not take the machine down to-morrow and test it in the barn?"

"Nothing could be better."

"There is a train to Eastbourne at one."

"I shall be at the station."

"Bring the gear with you, and I will bring the flanges," said the mechanician, rising. "To-morrow will prove whether we have been following a shadow, or whether fortune is at our feet. One o'clock at Victoria." He walked swiftly down the stair and was quickly reabsorbed into the flood of comfortless clammy humanity which ebbed and flowed along the Strand.

The morning was bright and spring-like. A pale blue sky arched over London, with a few gauzy white clouds drifting lazily across it. At eleven o'clock Brown might have been seen entering the Patent Office with a great roll of parchment, diagrams, and plans under his arm. At twelve he emerged again smiling, and, opening his pocket-book, he packed away very carefully a small slip of official blue paper. At five minutes to one his cab rolled into Victoria Station. Two giant canvas-covered parcels, like enormous kites, were handed down by the cabman from the top, and consigned to the care of a guard. On the platform Pericord was pacing up and down, with long, eager step and swinging arms, a tinge of pink upon his sunken and sallow cheeks.

"All right?" he asked.

Brown pointed in answer to his baggage.

"I have the motor and the girdle already packed away in the guard's van. Be careful, guard, for it is delicate machinery of great value. So! Now we can start with an easy conscience "

At Eastbourne the precious motor was carried to a four-wheeler, and the great flanges hoisted on the top. A long drive took them to the house where the keys were kept, whence they set off across the barren Downs. The building which was their destination was a commonplace whitewashed structure, with straggling stables and out-houses, standing in a grassy hollow which sloped down from the edge of the chalk cliffs. It was a cheerless house even when in use, but now with its smokeless chimneys and shuttered windows it looked doubly dreary. The owner had planted a grove of young larches and firs around it, but the sweeping spray had blighted them, and they hung their withered heads in melancholy groups. It was a gloomy and forbidding spot.

But the inventors were in no mood to be moved by such trifles. The lonelier the place, the more fitted for their purpose. With the help of the cabman they carried their packages down the footpath, and laid them in the darkened dining-room. The sun was setting as the distant murmur of wheels told them that they were finally alone.

Pericord had thrown open the shutters and the mellow evening light streamed in through the discoloured windows. Brown drew a knife from his pocket and cut the pack-thread with which the canvas was secured. As the brown covering fell away it disclosed two great yellow metal fans. These he leaned carefully against the wall. The girdle, the connecting-bands, and the motor were then in turn unpacked. It was dark before all was set out in order. A lamp was lit, and by its light the two men continued to tighten screws, clinch rivets, and make the last preparations for their experiment.

"That finishes it," said Brown at last, stepping back and surveying the machine.

Pericord said nothing, but his face glowed with pride and expectation.

"We must have something to eat," Brown remarked, laying out some provisions which he had brought with him.

"Afterwards."

"No, now," said the stolid mechanician. "I am half starved." He pulled up to the table and made a hearty meal, while his Celtic companion strode impatiently up and down, with twitching fingers and restless eyes.

"Now then," said Brown, facing round, and brushing the crumbs from his lap, "who is to put it on?"

"I shall," cried his companion eagerly. "What we do to-night is likely to be historic."

"But there is some danger," suggested Brown. "We cannot quite tell how it may act."

"That is nothing," said Pericord, with a wave of his hand.

"But there is no use our going out of our way to incur danger."

"What then? One of us must do it."

"Not at all. The motor would act equally well if attached to any inanimate object."

"That is true," said Pericord thoughtfully.

"There are bricks by the barn. I have a sack here. Why should not a bagful of them take our place?"

"It is a good idea. I see no objection."

"Come on then," and the two sallied out, bearing with them the various sections of their machine. The moon was shining cold and clear though an occasional ragged cloud drifted across her face. All was still and silent upon the Downs. They stood and listened before they entered the barn, but not a sound came to their ears, save the dull murmur of the sea and the distant barking of a dog. Pericord journeyed backwards and forwards with all that they might need, while Brown filled a long narrow sack with bricks.

When all was ready, the door of the barn was closed, and the lamp balanced upon an empty packing-case. The bag of bricks was laid upon two trestles, and the broad steel girdle was buckled round it. Then the great flanges, the wires, and the metal box containing the motor were in turn attached to the girdle. Last of all a flat steel rudder, shaped like a fish's tail, was secured to the bottom of the sack.

"We must make it travel in a small circle," said Pericord, glancing round at the bare high walls.

"Tie the rudder down at one side," suggested Brown. "Now it is ready. Press the connection and off she goes!"

Pericord leaned forward, his long sallow face quivering with excitement. His white nervous hands darted here and there among the wires. Brown stood impassive with critical eyes. There was a sharp burr from the machine. The huge yellow wings gave a convulsive flap. Then another. Then a third, slower and stronger, with a fuller sweep. Then a fourth which filled the barn with a blast of driven air. At the fifth the bag of bricks began to dance upon the trestles. At the sixth it sprang into the air, and would have fallen to the ground, but the seventh came to save it, and fluttered it forward through the air. Slowly rising, it flapped heavily round in a circle, like some great clumsy bird, filling the barn with its buzzing and whirring. In the uncertain yellow light of the single lamp it was strange to see the loom of the ungainly thing, flapping off into the shadows, and then circling back into the narrow zone of light.

The two men stood for a while in silence. Then Pericord threw his long arms up into the air.

"It acts!" he cried. "The Brown-Pericord Motor acts!" He danced about like a madman in his delight. Brown's eyes twinkled, and he began to whistle.

"See how smoothly it goes, Brown!" cried the inventor. "And the rudder—how well it acts! We must register it to-morrow."

His comrade's face darkened and set. "It is registered," he said, with a forced laugh.

"Registered?" said Pericord. "Registered?" He repeated the word first in a whisper, and then in a kind of scream. "Who has dared to register my invention?"

"I did it this morning. There is nothing to be excited about. It is all right."

"You registered the motor! Under whose name?"

"Under my own," said Brown sullenly. "I consider that I have the best right to it."

"And my name does not appear?"

"No, but——"

"You villain!" screamed Pericord. "You thief and villain! You would steal my work! You would filch my credit! I will have that patent back if I have to tear your throat out!" A sombre fire burned in his black eyes, and his hands writhed themselves together with passion. Brown was no coward, but he shrank back as the other advanced upon him.

"Keep your hands off!" he said, drawing a knife from his pocket. "I will defend myself if you attack me.

"You threaten me?" cried Pericord, whose face was livid with anger. "You are a bully as well as a cheat. Will you give up the patent?"

"No, I will not."

"Brown, I say, give it up!"

"I will not. I did the work."

Pericord sprang madly forward with blazing eyes and clutching fingers. His companion writhed out of his grasp, but was dashed against the packing-case, over which he fell. The lamp was extinguished, and the whole barn plunged into darkness. A single ray of moonlight shining through a narrow chink flickered over the great waving fans as they came and went.

"Will you give up the patent, Brown?"

There was no answer.

"Will you give it up?"

Again no answer. Not a sound save the humming and creaking overhead. A cold pang of fear and doubt struck through Pericord's heart. He felt aimlessly about in the dark and his fingers closed upon a hand. It was cold and unresponsive. With all his anger turned to icy horror he struck a match, set the lamp up, and lit it.

Brown lay huddled up on the other side of the packing-case. Pericord seized him in his arms, and with convulsive strength lifted him across. Then the mystery of his silence was explained. He had fallen with his right arm doubled up under him, and his own weight had driven the knife deeply into his body. He had died without a groan. The tragedy had been sudden, horrible, and complete.

Pericord sat silently on the edge of the case, staring blankly down, and shivering like one with the ague, while the great Brown-

Pericord Motor boomed and hurtled above him. How long he sat there can never be known. It might have been minutes or it might have been hours. A thousand mad schemes flashed through his dazed brain. It was true that he had been only the indirect cause. But who would believe that? He glanced down at his blood-spattered clothing. Everything was against him. It would be better to fly than to give himself up, relying upon his innocence. No one in London knew where they were. If he could dispose of the body he might have a few days clear before any suspicion would be aroused.

Suddenly a loud crash recalled him to himself. The flying sack had gradually risen with each successive circle until it had struck against the rafters. The blow displaced the connecting-gear, and the machine fell heavily to the ground. Pericord undid the girdle. The motor was uninjured. A sudden, strange thought flashed upon him as he looked at it. The machine had become hateful to him. He might dispose both of it and the body in a way that would baffle all human search.

He threw open the barn door, and carried his companion out into the moonlight. There was a hillock outside, and on the summit of this he laid him reverently down. Then he brought from the barn the motor, the girdle and the flanges. With trembling fingers he fastened the broad steel belt round the dead man's waist. Then he screwed the wings into the sockets. Beneath he slung the motor-box, fastened the wires, and switched on the connection. For a minute or two the huge yellow fans flapped and flickered. Then the body began to move in little jumps down the side of the hillock, gathering a gradual momentum, until at last it heaved up into the air and soared heavily off in the moonlight. He had not used the rudder, but had turned the head for the south. Gradually the weird thing rose higher, and sped faster, until it had passed over the line of cliff, and was sweeping over the silent sea. Pericord watched it with a white drawn face, until it looked like a black bird with golden wings half shrouded in the mist which lay over the waters.

In the New York State Lunatic Asylum there is a wild-eyed man whose name and birth-place are alike unknown. His reason has been unseated by some sudden shock, the doctors say, though of what nature they are unable to determine. "It is the most delicate machine which is most readily put out of gear," they remark, and point, in proof of their axiom, to the complicated electric engines, and remarkable aeronautic machines which the patient is fond of devising in his more lucid moments.

VI

THE SEALED ROOM

A solicitor of an active habit and athletic tastes who is compelled by his hopes of business to remain within the four walls of his office from ten till five must take what exercise he can in the evenings. Hence it was that I was in the habit of indulging in very long nocturnal excursions, in which I sought the heights of Hampstead and Highgate in order to cleanse my system from the impure air of Abchurch Lane. It was in the course of one of these aimless rambles that I first met Felix Stanniford, and so led up to what has been the most extraordinary adventure of my lifetime.

One evening—it was in April or early May of the year 1894—I made my way to the extreme northern fringe of London, and was walking down one of those fine avenues of high brick villas which the huge city is for ever pushing farther and farther out into the country. It was a fine, clear spring night, the moon was shining out of an unclouded sky, and I, having already left many miles behind me, was inclined to walk slowly and look about me. In this contemplative mood, my attention was arrested by one of the houses which I was passing.

It was a very large building, standing in its own grounds, a little back from the road. It was modern in appearance, and yet it was far less so than its neighbours, all of which were crudely and painfully new.

Their symmetrical line was broken by the gap caused by the laurel-studded lawn, with the great, dark, gloomy house looming at the back of it. Evidently it had been the country retreat of some wealthy merchant, built perhaps when the nearest street was a mile off, and now gradually overtaken and surrounded by the red brick tentacles of the London octopus. The next stage, I reflected, would be its digestion and absorption, so that the cheap builder might rear a dozen eighty-pound-a-year villas upon the garden frontage. And then, as all this passed vaguely through my mind, an incident occurred which brought my thoughts into quite another channel.

A four-wheeled cab, that opprobium of London, was coming jolting and creaking in one direction, while in the other there was a yellow glare from the lamp of a cyclist. They were the only moving objects in the whole long, moonlit road, and yet they crashed into each other with that malignant accuracy which brings two ocean liners together in the broad waste of the Atlantic. It was the cyclist's fault. He tried to cross in front of the cab, miscalculated his distance, and was knocked sprawling by the horse's shoulder. He rose, snarling; the cabman swore back at him, and then, realising that his number had not yet been taken, lashed his horse and lumbered off. The cyclist caught at the handles of his prostrate machine, and then suddenly sat down with a groan. "Oh, Lord!" he said.

I ran across the road to his side. "Any harm done?" I asked.

"It's my ankle," said he. "Only a twist, I think; but it's pretty painful. Just give me your hand, will you?"

He lay in the yellow circle of the cycle lamp, and I noted as I helped him to his feet that he was a gentlemanly young fellow, with a slight dark moustache and large, brown eyes, sensitive and nervous in appearance, with indications of weak health upon his sunken cheeks. Work or worry had left its traces upon his thin, yellow face. He stood up when I pulled his hand, but he held one foot in the air, and he groaned as he moved it.

"I can't put it to the ground," said he.

"Where do you live?"

"Here!" he nodded his head towards the big, dark house in the garden. "I was cutting across to the gate when that confounded cab ran into me. Could you help me so far?"

It was easily done. I put his cycle inside the gate, and then I supported him down the drive, and up the steps to the hall door. There was not a light anywhere, and the place was as black and silent as if no one had ever lived in it.

"That will do. Thank you very much," said he, fumbling with his key in the lock.

"No, you must allow me to see you safe."

He made some feeble, petulant protest, and then realised that he could really do nothing without me. The door had opened into a pitch-dark hall. He lurched forward, with my hand still on his arm.

"This door to the right," said he, feeling about in the darkness.

I opened the door, and at the same moment he managed to strike a light. There was a lamp upon the table, and we lit it between us. "Now, I'm all right. You can leave me now! Good-bye!" said he, and with the words he sat down in the arm-chair and fainted dead away.

It was a queer position for me. The fellow looked so ghastly, that really I was not sure that he was not dead. Presently his lips quivered and his breast heaved, but his eyes were two white slits and his colour was horrible. The responsibility was more than I could stand. I pulled at the bell-rope, and heard the bell ringing furiously far away. But no one came in response. The bell tinkled away into silence, which no murmur or movement came to break. I waited, and rang again, with the same result. There must be some one about. This young gentleman could not live all alone in that huge house. His people ought to know of his condition. If they would not answer the bell, I must hunt them out myself. I seized the lamp and rushed from the room.

What I saw outside amazed me. The hall was empty. The stairs were bare, and yellow with dust. There were three doors opening into spacious rooms, and each was uncarpeted and undraped, save for the grey webs which drooped from the cornice, and rosettes of lichen which had formed upon the walls. My feet reverberated in those empty and silent chambers. Then I wandered on down the passage, with the idea that the kitchens, at least, might be tenanted. Some caretaker might lurk in some secluded room. No, they were all equally desolate. Despairing of finding any help, I ran down another corridor, and came on something which surprised me more than ever.

The passage ended in a large, brown door, and the door had a seal of red wax the size of a five-shilling piece over the key-hole. This seal gave me the impression of having been there for a long time, for it was dusty and discoloured. I was still staring at it, and wondering what that door might conceal, when I heard a voice calling behind me, and, running back, found my young man sitting up in his chair and very much astonished at finding himself in darkness.

"Why on earth did you take the lamp away?" he asked.

"I was looking for assistance."

"You might look for some time," said he. "I am alone in the house."

"Awkward if you get an illness."

"It was foolish of me to faint. I inherit a weak heart from my mother, and pain or emotion has that effect upon me. It will carry me off some day, as it did her. You're not a doctor, are you?"

"No, a lawyer. Frank Alder is my name."

"Mine is Felix Stanniford. Funny that I should meet a lawyer, for my friend, Mr. Perceval, was saying that we should need one soon."

"Very happy, I am sure."

"Well, that will depend upon him, you know. Did you say that you had run with that lamp all over the ground floor?"

"Yes."

"All over it?" he asked, with emphasis, and he looked at me very hard.

"I think so. I kept on hoping that I should find some one."

"Did you enter all the rooms?" he asked, with the same intent gaze.

"Well, all that I could enter."

"Oh, then you did notice it!" said he, and he shrugged his shoulders with the air of a man who makes the best of a bad job.

"Notice, what?"

"Why, the door with the seal on it."

"Yes, I did."

"Weren't you curious to know what was in it?"

"Well, it did strike me as unusual."

"Do you think you could go on living alone in this house, year after year, just longing all the time to know what is at the other side of that door, and yet not looking?"

"Do you mean to say," I cried, "that you don't know yourself?"

"No more than you do."

"Then why don't you look?"

"I mustn't," said he.

He spoke in a constrained way, and I saw that I had blundered on to some delicate ground. I don't know that I am more inquisitive than my neighbours, but there certainly was something in the situation which appealed very strongly to my curiosity. However, my last excuse for remaining in the house was gone now that my companion had recovered his senses. I rose to go.

"Are you in a hurry?" he asked.

"No; I have nothing to do."

"Well, I should be very glad if you would stay with me a little. The fact is that I live a very retired and secluded life here. I don't suppose there is a man in London who leads such a life as I do. It is quite unusual for me to have any one to talk with."

I looked round at the little room, scantily furnished, with a sofa-bed at one side. Then I thought of the great, bare house, and the sinister door with the discoloured red seal upon it. There was something queer and grotesque in the situation, which made me long to know a little more. Perhaps I should, if I waited. I told him that I should be very happy.

"You will find the spirits and a siphon upon the side table. You must forgive me if I cannot act as host, but I can't get across the room. Those are cigars in the tray there. I'll take one myself, I think. And so you are a solicitor, Mr. Alder?"

"Yes."

"And I am nothing. I am that most helpless of living creatures, the son of a millionaire. I was brought up with the expectation of great wealth; and here I am, a poor man, without any profession at all. And then, on the top of it all, I am left with this great mansion on my hands, which I cannot possibly keep up. Isn't it an absurd situation? For me to use this as my dwelling is like a coster drawing his barrow with a thoroughbred. A donkey would be more useful to him, and a cottage to me."

"But why not sell the house?" I asked.

"I mustn't."

"Let it, then?"

"No, I mustn't do that either."

I looked puzzled, and my companion smiled.

"I'll tell you how it is, if it won't bore you," said he.

"On the contrary, I should be exceedingly interested."

"I think, after your kind attention to me, I cannot do less than relieve any curiosity that you may feel. You must know that my father was Stanislaus Stanniford, the banker."

Stanniford, the banker! I remembered the name at once. His flight from the country some seven years before had been one of the scandals and sensations of the time.

"I see that you remember," said my companion. "My poor father left the country to avoid numerous friends, whose savings he had invested in an unsuccessful speculation. He was a nervous, sensitive man, and the responsibility quite upset his reason. He had committed no legal offence. It was purely a matter of sentiment. He would not even face his own family, and he died among strangers without ever letting us know where he was."

"He died!" said I.

"We could not prove his death, but we know that it must be so, because the speculations came right again, and so there was no reason why he should not look any man in the face. He would have returned if he were alive. But he must have died in the last two years."

"Why in the last two years?"

"Because we heard from him two years ago."

"Did he not tell you then where he was living?"

"The letter came from Paris, but no address was given. It was when my poor mother died. He wrote to me then, with some instructions and some advice, and I have never heard from him since."

"Had you heard before?"

"Oh, yes, we had heard before, and that's where our mystery of the sealed door, upon which you stumbled to-night, has its origin. Pass me that desk, if you please. Here I have my father's letters, and you are the first man except Mr. Perceval who has seen them."

"Who is Mr. Perceval, may I ask?"

"He was my father's confidential clerk, and he has continued to be the friend and adviser of my mother and then of myself. I don't know what we should have done without Perceval. He saw the letters, but no one else. This is the first one, which came on the very day when my father fled, seven years ago. Read it to yourself."

This is the letter which I read:

"My Ever Dearest Wife,—

"Since Sir William told me how weak your heart is, and how harmful any shock might be, I have never talked about my business affairs to you. The time has come when at all risks I can no longer refrain from telling you that things have been going badly with me. This will cause me to leave you for a little time, but it is with the absolute assurance that we shall see each other very soon. On this you can thoroughly rely. Our parting is only for a very short time, my own darling, so don't let it fret you, and above all don't let it impair your health, for that is what I want above all things to avoid.

"Now, I have a request to make, and I implore you by all that binds us together to fulfil it exactly as I tell you. There are some things which I do not wish to be seen by any one in my dark room—the room which I use for photographic purposes at the end of the garden passage. To prevent any painful thoughts, I may assure you once for all, dear, that it is nothing of which I need be ashamed. But still I do not wish you or Felix to enter that room. It is locked, and I implore you when you receive this to at once place a seal over the lock, and leave it so. Do not sell or let the house, for in either case my secret will be discovered. As long as you or Felix are in the house, I know that you will comply with my wishes. When Felix is twenty-one he may enter the room—not before.

"And now, good-bye, my own best of wives. During our short separation you can consult Mr. Perceval on any matters which may arise. He has my complete confidence. I hate to leave Felix and you—even for a time—but there is really no choice.

"Ever and always your loving husband,

"Stanislaus Stanniford.

"June 4th, 1887."

"These are very private family matters for me to inflict upon you," said my companion apologetically. "You must look upon it as done in your professional capacity. I have wanted to speak about it for years."

"I am honoured by your confidence," I answered, "and exceedingly interested by the facts."

"My father was a man who was noted for his almost morbid love of truth. He was always pedantically accurate. When he said, therefore, that he hoped to see my mother very soon, and when he said that he had nothing to be ashamed of in that dark room, you may rely upon it that he meant it."

"Then what can it be?" I ejaculated.

"Neither my mother nor I could imagine. We carried out his wishes to the letter, and placed the seal upon the door; there it has been ever since. My mother lived for five years after my father's disappearance, although at the time all the doctors said that she could not survive long. Her heart was terribly diseased. During the first few months she had two letters from my father. Both had the Paris postmark, but no address. They were short and to the same effect: that they would soon be re-united, and that she should not fret. Then there was a silence, which lasted until her death; and then came a letter to me of so private a nature that I cannot show it to you, begging me never to think evil of him, giving me much good advice, and saying that the sealing of the room was of less importance now than during the lifetime of my mother, but that the opening might still cause pain to others, and that, therefore, he thought it best that it should be postponed until my twenty-first year, for the lapse of time would make things easier. In the meantime, he committed the care of the room to me; so now you can understand how it is that, although I am a very poor man, I can neither let nor sell this great house."

"You could mortgage it."

"My father had already done so."

"It is a most singular state of affairs."

"My mother and I were gradually compelled to sell the furniture and to dismiss the servants, until now, as you see, I am living unattended in a single room. But I have only two more months."

"What do you mean?"

"Why, that in two months I come of age. The first thing that I do will be to open that door; the second, to get rid of the house."

"Why should your father have continued to stay away when these investments had recovered themselves?"

"He must be dead."

"You say that he had not committed any legal offence when he fled the country?"

"None."

"Why should he not take your mother with him?"

"I do not know."

"Why should he conceal his address?"

"I do not know."

"Why should he allow your mother to die and be buried without coming back?"

"I do not know."

"My dear sir," said I, "if I may speak with the frankness of a professional adviser, I should say that it is very clear that your father had the strongest reasons for keeping out of the country, and that, if nothing has been proved against him, he at least thought that something might be, and refused to put himself within the power of the law. Surely that must be obvious, for in what other possible way can the facts be explained?"

My companion did not take my suggestion in good part.

"You had not the advantage of knowing my father, Mr. Alder," he said coldly. "I was only a boy when he left us, but I shall always look upon him as my ideal man. His only fault was that he was too sensitive and too unselfish. That any one should lose money through him would cut him to the heart. His sense of honour was most acute, any theory of his disappearance which conflicts with that is a mistaken one."

It pleased me to hear the lad speak out so roundly, and yet I knew that the facts were against him, and that he was incapable of taking an unprejudiced view of the situation.

"I only speak as an outsider," said I. "And now I must leave you, for I have a long walk before me. Your story has interested me so much that I should be glad if you could let me know the sequel."

"Leave me your card," said he; and so, having bade him "good-night," I left him.

I heard nothing more of the matter for some time, and had almost feared that it would prove to be one of those fleeting experiences which drift away from our direct observation and end only in a hope or a suspicion. One afternoon, however, a card bearing the name of Mr. J. H. Perceval was brought up to my office in Abchurch Lane, and its bearer, a small, dry, bright-eyed fellow of fifty, was ushered in by the clerk.

"I believe, sir," said he, "that my name has been mentioned to you by my young friend, Mr. Felix Stanniford?"

"Of course," I answered, "I remember."

"He spoke to you, I understand, about the circumstances in connection with the disappearance of my former employer, Mr. Stanislaus Stanniford, and the existence of a sealed room in his former residence."

"He did."

"And you expressed an interest in the matter."

"It interested me extremely."

"You are aware that we hold Mr. Stanniford's permission to open the door on the twenty-first birthday of his son?"

"I remember."

"The twenty-first birthday is to-day."

"Have you opened it?" I asked eagerly.

"Not yet, sir," said he gravely. "I have reason to believe that it would be well to have witnesses present when that door is opened. You are a lawyer, and you are acquainted with the facts. Will you be present on the occasion?"

"Most certainly."

"You are employed during the day, and so am I. Shall we meet at nine o'clock at the house?"

"I will come with pleasure."

"Then you will find us waiting for you. Good-bye, for the present." He bowed solemnly, and took his leave.

I kept my appointment that evening, with a brain which was weary with fruitless attempts to think out some plausible explanation of the mystery which we were about to solve. Mr. Perceval and my young acquaintance were waiting for me in the little room. I was not surprised to see the young man looking pale and nervous, but I was rather astonished to find the dry little City man in a state of intense, though partially suppressed, excitement. His cheeks were flushed, his hands twitching, and he could not stand still for an instant.

Stanniford greeted me warmly, and thanked me many times for having come. "And now, Perceval," said he to his companion, "I suppose there is no obstacle to our putting the thing through without delay? I shall be glad to get it over."

The banker's clerk took up the lamp and led the way. But he paused in the passage outside the door, and his hand was shaking, so that the light flickered up and down the high, bare walls.

"Mr. Stanniford," said he, in a cracking voice, "I hope you will prepare yourself in case any shock should be awaiting you when that seal is removed and the door is opened."

"What could there be, Perceval? You are trying to frighten me."

"No, Mr. Stanniford; but I should wish you to be ready ... to be braced up ... not to allow yourself ..." He had to lick his dry lips between every jerky sentence, and I suddenly realised, as clearly as if he had told me, that he knew what was behind that closed door, and that it was something terrible. "Here are the keys, Mr. Stanniford, but remember my warning!"

He had a bunch of assorted keys in his hand, and the young man snatched them from him. Then he thrust a knife under the discoloured seal and jerked it off. The lamp was rattling and shaking in Perceval's hands, so I took it from him and held it near the key-hole, while Stanniford tried key after key. At last one turned in the lock, the door flew open, he took one step into the room, and then, with a horrible cry, the young man fell senseless at our feet.

If I had not given heed to the clerk's warning, and braced myself for a shock, I should certainly have dropped the lamp. The room, windowless and bare, was fitted up as a photographic laboratory, with a tap and sink at the side of it. A shelf of bottles and measures stood at one side, and a peculiar, heavy smell, partly chemical, partly animal, filled the air. A single table and chair were in front of us, and at this, with his back turned towards us, a man was seated in the act of writing. His outline and attitude were as natural as life; but as the light fell upon him, it made my hair rise to see that the nape of his neck was black and wrinkled, and no thicker than my wrist. Dust lay upon him—thick, yellow dust—upon his hair, his shoulders, his shrivelled, lemon-coloured hands. His head had fallen forward upon his breast. His pen still rested upon a discoloured sheet of paper.

"My poor master! My poor, poor master!" cried the clerk, and the tears were running down his cheeks.

"What!" I cried, "Mr. Stanislaus Stanniford!"

"Here he has sat for seven years. Oh, why would he do it? I begged him, I implored him, I went on my knees to him, but he would have his way. You see the key on the table. He had locked the door upon the inside. And he has written something. We must take it."

"Yes, yes, take it, and for God's sake, let us get out of this," I cried; "the air is poisonous. Come, Stanniford, come!" Taking an arm each, we half led and half carried the terrified man back to his own room.

"It was my father!" he cried, as he recovered his consciousness. "He is sitting there dead in his chair. You knew it, Perceval! This was what you meant when you warned me."

"Yes, I knew it, Mr. Stanniford. I have acted for the best all along, but my position has been a terribly difficult one. For seven years I have known that your father was dead in that room."

"You knew it, and never told us!"

"Don't be harsh with me, Mr. Stanniford, sir! Make allowance for a man who has had a hard part to play."

"My head is swimming round. I cannot grasp it!" He staggered up, and helped himself from the brandy bottle. "These letters to my mother and to myself—were they forgeries?"

"No, sir; your father wrote them and addressed them, and left them in my keeping to be posted. I have followed his instructions to the very letter in all things. He was my master, and I have obeyed him."

The brandy had steadied the young man's shaken nerves. "Tell me about it. I can stand it now," said he.

"Well, Mr. Stanniford, you know that at one time there came a period of great trouble upon your father, and he thought that many poor people were about to lose their savings through his fault. He was a man who was so tender-hearted that he could not bear the thought. It worried him and tormented him, until he determined to end his life. Oh, Mr. Stanniford, if you knew how I have prayed him and wrestled with him over it, you would never blame me! And he in turn prayed me as no man has ever prayed me before. He had made up his mind, and he would do it in any case, he said; but it rested with me whether his death should be happy and easy or whether it should be most miserable. I read in his eyes that he meant what he said. And at last I yielded to his prayers, and I consented to do his will.

"What was troubling him was this. He had been told by the first doctor in London that his wife's heart would fail at the slightest shock. He had a horror of accelerating her end, and yet his own existence had become unendurable to him. How could he end himself without injuring her?

"You know now the course that he took. He wrote the letter which she received. There was nothing in it which was not literally true. When he spoke of seeing her again so soon, he was referring to her own approaching death, which he had been assured could not be delayed more than a very few months. So convinced was he of this, that he only left two letters to be forwarded at intervals after his death. She lived five years, and I had no letters to send.

"He left another letter with me to be sent to you, sir, upon the occasion of the death of your mother. I posted all these in Paris to sustain the idea of his being abroad. It was his wish that I should say nothing, and I have said nothing. I have been a faithful servant. Seven years after his death, he thought no doubt that the shock to the feelings of his surviving friends Would be lessened. He was always considerate for others."

There was a silence for some time. It was broken by young Stanniford.

"I cannot blame you, Perceval. You have spared my mother a shock, which would certainly have broken her heart. What is that paper?"

"It is what your father was writing, sir. Shall I read it to you?"

"Do so."

"'I have taken the poison, and I feel it working in my veins. It is strange, but not painful. When these words are read I shall, if my wishes have been faithfully carried out, have been dead many years. Surely no one who has lost money through me will still bear me animosity. And you, Felix, you will forgive me this family scandal. May God find rest for a sorely wearied spirit!'"

"Amen!" we cried, all three.

VII

A PHYSIOLOGIST'S WIFE

Professor Ainslie Grey had not come down to breakfast at the usual hour. The presentation chiming-clock which stood between the terra-cotta busts of Claude Bernard and of John Hunter upon the dining-room mantelpiece had rung out the half-hour and the three-quarters. Now its golden hand was verging upon the nine, and yet there were no signs of the master of the house.

It was an unprecedented occurrence. During the twelve years that she had kept house for him, his younger sister had never known him a second behind his time. She sat now in front of the high silver coffee-pot, uncertain whether to order the gong to be resounded or to wait on in silence. Either course might be a mistake. Her brother was not a man who permitted mistakes.

Miss Ainslie Grey was rather above the middle height, thin, with peering, puckered eyes, and the rounded shoulders which mark the bookish woman. Her face was long and spare, flecked with colour above the cheek-bones, with a reasonable, thoughtful forehead, and a dash of absolute obstinacy in her thin lips and prominent chin. Snow-white cuffs and collar, with a plain dark dress, cut with almost Quaker-like simplicity, bespoke the primness of her taste. An ebony cross hung over her flattened chest. She sat very upright in her chair, listening with raised eyebrows, and swinging her eyeglasses backwards and forwards with a nervous gesture which was peculiar to her.

Suddenly she gave a sharp, satisfied jerk of the head, and began to pour out the coffee. From outside there came the dull thudding sound of heavy feet Upon thick carpet. The door swung open, and the Professor entered with a quick, nervous step. He nodded to his sister, and seating himself at the other side of the table, began to open the small pile of letters which lay beside his plate.

Professor Ainslie Grey was at that time forty-three years of age— nearly twelve years older than his sister. His career had been a brilliant one. At Edinburgh, at Cambridge, and at Vienna he had laid the foundations of his great reputation, both in physiology and in zoology.

His pamphlet, "On the Mesoblastic Origin of Excitomotor Nerve Roots," had won him his fellowship of the Royal Society; and his researches, "Upon the Nature of Bathybius, with some Remarks upon Lithococci," had been translated into at least three European languages. He had been referred to by one of the greatest living authorities as being the very type and embodiment of all that was best in modern science. No wonder, then, that when the commercial city of Birchespool decided to create a medical school, they were only too glad to confer the chair of physiology upon Mr.

Ainslie Grey. They valued him the more from the conviction that their class was only one step in his upward journey, and that the first vacancy would remove him to some more illustrious seat of learning.

In person he was not unlike his sister. The same eyes, the same contour, the same intellectual forehead. His lips, however, were firmer, and his long, thin lower jaw was sharper and more decided. He ran his finger and thumb down it from time to time, as he glanced over his letters.

"These maids are very noisy," he remarked, as a clack of tongues sounded in the distance.

"It is Sarah," said his sister; "I shall speak about it."

She had handed over his coffee-cup, and was sipping at her own, glancing furtively through her narrowed lids at the austere face of her brother.

"The first great advance of the human race," said the Professor, "was when, by the development of their left frontal convolutions, they attained the power of speech. Their second advance was when they learned to control that power. Woman has not yet attained the second stage."

He half closed his eyes as he spoke, and thrust his chin forward, but as he ceased he had a trick of suddenly opening both eyes very wide and staring sternly at his interlocutor.

"I am not garrulous, John," said his sister.

"No, Ada; in many respects you approach the superior or male type."

The Professor bowed over his egg with the manner of one who utters a courtly compliment; but the lady pouted, and gave an impatient little shrug of her shoulders.

"You were late this morning, John," she remarked, after a pause.

"Yes, Ada; I slept badly. Some little cerebral congestion, no doubt due to over-stimulation of the centres of thought. I have been a little disturbed in my mind."

His sister stared across at him in astonishment. The Professor's mental processes had hitherto been as regular as his habits. Twelve years' continual intercourse had taught her that he lived in a serene and rarefied atmosphere of scientific calm, high above the petty emotions which affect humbler minds.

"You are surprised, Ada," he remarked. "Well, I cannot wonder at it. I should have been surprised myself if I had been told that I was so sensitive to vascular influences. For, after all, all disturbances are vascular if you probe them deep enough. I am thinking of getting married."

"Not Mrs. O'James?" cried Ada Grey, laying down her egg-spoon.

"My dear, you have the feminine quality of receptivity very remarkably developed. Mrs. O'James is the lady in question."

"But you know so little of her. The Esdailes themselves know so little. She is really only an acquaintance, although she is staying at The Lindens. Would it not be wise to speak to Mrs. Esdaile first, John?"

"I do not think, Ada, that Mrs. Esdaile is at all likely to say anything which would materially affect my course of action. I have given the matter due consideration. The scientific mind is slow at arriving at conclusions, but having once formed them, it is not prone to change. Matrimony is the natural condition of the human race. I have, as you know, been so engaged in academical and other work, that I have had no time to devote to merely personal questions. It is different now, and I see no valid reason why I should forego this opportunity of seeking a suitable helpmate."

"And you are engaged?"

"Hardly that, Ada. I ventured yesterday to indicate to the lady that I was prepared to submit to the common lot of humanity. I shall wait upon her after my morning lecture, and learn how far my proposals meet with her acquiescence. But you frown, Ada!"

His sister started, and made an effort to conceal her expression of annoyance. She even stammered out some few words of congratulation, but a vacant look had come into her brother's eyes, and he was evidently not listening to her.

"I am sure, John," she said, "that I wish you the happiness which you deserve. If I hesitated at all, it is because I know how much is at stake, and because the thing is so sudden, so unexpected." Her thin white hand stole up to the black cross upon her bosom. "These are moments when we need guidance, John. If I could persuade you to turn to spiritual——"

The Professor waved the suggestion away with a deprecating hand.

"It is useless to reopen that question," he said. "We cannot argue upon it. You assume more than I can grant. I am forced to dispute your premises. We have no common basis."

His sister sighed.

"You have no faith," she said.

"I have faith in those great evolutionary forces which are leading the human race to some unknown but elevated goal."

"You believe in nothing."

"On the contrary, my dear Ada, I believe in the differentiation of protoplasm."

She shook her head sadly. It was the one subject upon which she ventured to dispute her brother's infallibility.

"This is rather beside the question," remarked the Professor, folding up his napkin. "If I am not mistaken, there is some possibility of another matrimonial event occurring in the family. Eh, Ada? What!"

His small eyes glittered with sly facetiousness as he shot a twinkle at his sister. She sat very stiff, and traced patterns upon the cloth with the sugar-tongs.

"Dr. James M'Murdo O'Brien——" said the Professor sonorously.

"Don't, John, don't!" cried Miss Ainslie Grey.

"Dr. James M'Murdo O'Brien," continued her brother inexorably, "is a man who has already made his mark upon the science of the day. He is my first and my most distinguished pupil. I assure you, Ada, that his 'Remarks upon the Bile-Pigments, with special reference to Urobilin,' is likely to live as a classic. It is not too much to say that he has revolutionised our views about Urobilin."

He paused, but his sister sat silent, with bent head and flushed cheeks. The little ebony cross rose and fell with her hurried breathings.

"Dr. James M'Murdo O'Brien has, as you know, the offer of the physiological chair at Melbourne. He has been in Australia five years, and has a brilliant future before him. To-day he leaves us for Edinburgh, and in two months' time he goes out to take over his new duties. You know his feeling towards you. It rests with you as to whether he goes out alone. Speaking for myself, I cannot imagine any higher mission for a woman of culture than to go through life in the company of a man who is capable of such a research as that which Dr. James M'Murdo O'Brien has brought to a successful conclusion."

"He has not spoken to me," murmured the lady.

"Ah, there are signs which are more subtle than speech," said her brother, wagging his head. "You are pale. Your vasomotor system is excited. Your arterioles have contracted. Let me entreat you to compose yourself. I think I hear the carriage. I fancy that you may have a visitor this morning, Ada. You will excuse me now."

With a quick glance at the clock he strode off into the hall, and within a few minutes he was rattling in his quiet, well-appointed brougham through the brick-lined streets of Birchespool.

His lecture over, Professor Ainslie Grey paid a visit to his laboratory, where he adjusted several scientific instruments, made a note as to the progress of three separate infusions of bacteria, cut half a dozen sections with a microtome, and finally resolved the difficulties of seven different gentlemen, who were pursuing researches in as many separate lines of inquiry. Having thus conscientiously and methodically completed the routine of his duties, he returned to his carriage and ordered the coachman to drive him to The Lindens. His face as he drove was cold and impassive, but he drew his fingers from time to time down his prominent chin with a jerky, twitchy movement.

The Lindens was an old-fashioned, ivy-clad house which had once been in the country, but was now caught in the long, red-brick feelers of the growing city. It still stood back from the road in the privacy of its own grounds. A winding path, lined with laurel bushes, led to the arched and porticoed entrance. To the right was a lawn, and at the far side, under the shadow of a hawthorn, a lady sat in a garden-chair with a book in her hands. At the click of the gate she started, and the Professor, catching sight of her, turned away from the door, and strode in her direction.

"What! won't you go in and see Mrs. Esdaile?" she asked, sweeping out from under the shadow of the hawthorn.

She was a small woman, strongly feminine, from the rich coils of her light-coloured hair to the dainty garden slipper which peeped from under her cream-tinted dress. One tiny well-gloved hand was outstretched in greeting, while the other pressed a thick, green-covered volume against her side. Her decision and quick, tactful manner bespoke the mature woman of the world; but her upraised face had preserved a girlish and even infantile expression of innocence in its large, fearless grey eyes, and sensitive, humorous mouth. Mrs. O'James was a widow, and she was two-and-thirty years of age; but neither fact could have been deduced from her appearance.

"You will surely go in and see Mrs. Esdaile," she repeated, glancing up at him with eyes which had in them something between a challenge and a caress.

"I did not come to see Mrs. Esdaile," he answered, with no relaxation of his cold and grave manner; "I came to see you."

"I am sure I should be highly honoured," she said, with just the slightest little touch of brogue in her accent. "What are the students to do without their Professor?"

"I have already completed my academic duties. Take my arm, and we shall walk in the sunshine. Surely we cannot wonder that Eastern people should have made a deity of the sun. It is the great beneficent force of Nature—man's ally against cold, sterility, and all that is abhorrent to him. What were you reading?"

"Hale's Matter and Life."

The Professor raised his thick eyebrows.

"Hale!" he said, and then again in a kind of whisper, "Hale!"

"You differ from him?" she asked.

"It is not I who differ from him. I am only a monad—a thing of no moment. The whole tendency of the highest plane of modern thought differs from him. He defends the indefensible. He is an excellent observer, but a feeble reasoner. I should not recommend you to found your conclusions upon 'Hale.'"

"I must read Nature's Chronicle to counteract his pernicious influence," said Mrs. O'James, with a soft, cooing laugh.

Nature's Chronicle was one of the many books in which Professor Ainslie Grey had enforced the negative doctrines of scientific agnosticism.

"It is a faulty work," said he; "I cannot recommend it. I would rather refer you to the standard writings of some of my older and more eloquent colleagues."

There was a pause in their talk as they paced up and down on the green, velvet-like lawn in the genial sunshine.

"Have you thought at all," he asked at last, "of the matter upon which I spoke to you last night?"

She said nothing, but walked by his side with her eyes averted and her face aslant.

"I would not hurry you unduly," he continued. "I know that it is a matter which can scarcely be decided off-hand. In my own case, it cost me some thought before I ventured to make the suggestion. I am not an emotional man, but I am conscious in your presence of the great evolutionary instinct which makes either sex the complement of the other."

"You believe in love, then?" she asked, with a twinkling, upward glance.

"I am forced to."

"And yet you can deny the soul?"

"How far these questions are psychic and how far material is still sub judice," said the Professor, with an air of toleration. "Protoplasm may prove to be the physical basis of love as well as of life."

"How inflexible you are!" she exclaimed; "you would draw love down to the level of physics."

"Or draw physics up to the level of love."

"Come, that is much better," she cried, with her sympathetic laugh. "That is really very pretty, and puts science in quite a delightful light."

Her eyes sparkled, and she tossed her chin with a pretty, wilful air of a woman who is mistress of the situation.

"I have reason to believe," said the Professor, "that my position here will prove to be only a stepping-stone to some wider scene of scientific activity. Yet, even here, my chair brings me in some fifteen hundred pounds a year, which is supplemented by a few hundreds from my books. I should therefore be in a position to provide you with those comforts to which you are accustomed. So much for my pecuniary position. As to my constitution, it has always been sound. I have never suffered from any illness in my life, save fleeting attacks of cephalalgia, the result of too prolonged a stimulation of the centres of cerebration. My father and mother had no sign of any morbid diathesis, but I will not conceal from you that my grandfather was afflicted with podagra."

Mrs. O'James looked startled.

"Is that very serious?" she asked.

"It is gout," said the Professor.

"Oh, is that all? It sounded much worse than that."

"It is a grave taint, but I trust that I shall not be a victim to atavism. I have laid these facts before you because they are factors which cannot be overlooked in forming your decision. May I ask now whether you see your way to accepting my proposal?"

He paused in his walk, and looked earnestly and expectantly down at her.

A struggle was evidently going on in her mind. Her eyes were cast down, her little slipper tapped the lawn, and her fingers played nervously with her chatelain. Suddenly, with a sharp, quick gesture which had in it something of abandon and recklessness, she held out her hand to her companion.

"I accept," she said.

They were standing under the shadow of the hawthorn. He stooped gravely down, and kissed her glove-covered fingers.

"I trust that you may never have cause to regret your decision," he said.

"I trust that you never may," she cried, with a heaving breast.

There were tears in her eyes, and her lips twitched with some strong emotion.

"Come into the sunshine again," said he. "It is the great restorative. Your nerves are shaken. Some little congestion of the medulla and pons. It is always instructive to reduce psychic or emotional conditions to their physical equivalents. You feel that your anchor is still firm in a bottom of ascertained fact."

"But it is so dreadfully unromantic," said Mrs. O'James, with her old twinkle.

"Romance is the offspring of imagination and of ignorance. Where science throws her calm, clear light there is happily no room for romance."

"But is not love romance?" she asked.

"Not at all. Love has been taken away from the poets, and has been brought within the domain of true science. It may prove to be one of the great cosmic elementary forces. When the atom of hydrogen draws the atom of chlorine towards it to form the perfected molecule of hydrochloric acid, the force which it exerts may be intrinsically similar to that which draws me to you. Attraction and repulsion appear to be the primary forces. This is attraction."

"And here is repulsion," said Mrs. O'James, as a stout, florid lady came sweeping across the lawn in their direction. "So glad you have come out, Mrs. Esdaile! Here is Professor Grey."

"How do you do, Professor?" said the lady, with some little pomposity of manner. "You were very wise to stay out here on so lovely a day. Is it not heavenly?"

"It is certainly very fine weather," the Professor answered.

"Listen to the wind sighing in the trees!" cried Mrs. Esdaile, holding up one finger. "It is Nature's lullaby. Could you not imagine it, Professor Grey, to be the whisperings of angels?"

"The idea had not occurred to me, madam."

"Ah, Professor, I have always the same complaint against you. A want of rapport with the deeper meanings of Nature. Shall I say a want of imagination? You do not feel an emotional thrill at the singing of that thrush?"

"I confess that I am not conscious of one, Mrs. Esdaile."

"Or at the delicate tint of that background of leaves? See the rich greens!"

"Chlorophyll," murmured the Professor.

"Science is so hopelessly prosaic. It dissects and labels, and loses sight of the great things in its attention to the little ones. You have a poor opinion of woman's intellect, Professor Grey. I think that I have heard you say so."

"It is a question of avoirdupois," said the Professor, closing his eyes and shrugging his shoulders. "The female cerebrum averages two ounces less in weight than the male. No doubt there are exceptions. Nature is always elastic."

"But the heaviest thing is not always the strongest," said Mrs. O'James, laughing. "Isn't there a law of compensation in science? May we not hope to make up in quality what we lack in quantity?"

"I think not," remarked the Professor gravely. "But there is your luncheon-gong. No, thank you, Mrs. Esdaile, I cannot stay. My carriage is waiting. Good-bye. Good-bye, Mrs. O'James."

He raised his hat and stalked slowly away among the laurel bushes.

"He has no taste," said Mrs. Esdaile—"no eye for beauty."

"On, the contrary," Mrs. O'James answered, with a saucy little jerk of the chin. "He has just asked me to be his wife."

As Professor Ainslie Grey ascended the steps of his house, the hall-door opened and a dapper gentleman stepped briskly out. He was somewhat sallow in the face, with dark, beady eyes, and a short, black beard with an aggressive bristle. Thought and work had left their traces upon his face, but he moved with the brisk activity of a man who had not yet bade good-bye to his youth.

"I'm in luck's way," he cried. "I wanted to see you."

"Then come back into the library," said the Professor; "you must stay and have lunch with us."

The two men entered the hall, and the Professor led the way into his private sanctum. He motioned his companion into an arm-chair.

"I trust that you have been successful, O'Brien," said he. "I should be loath to exercise any undue pressure upon my sister Ada; but I have given her to understand that there is no one whom I should prefer for a brother-in-law to my most brilliant scholar, the author of 'Some Remarks upon the Bile-Pigments, with special reference to Urobilin.'"

"You are very kind, Professor Grey—you have always been very kind," said the other. "I approached Miss Grey upon the subject; she did not say No."

"She said Yes, then?"

"No; she proposed to leave the matter open until my return from Edinburgh. I go to-day, as you know, and I hope to commence my research to-morrow."

"On the comparative anatomy of the vermiform appendix, by James M'Murdo O'Brien," said the Professor sonorously. "It is a glorious subject—a subject which lies at the very root of evolutionary philosophy."

"Ah, she is the dearest girl," cried O'Brien, with a sudden little spurt of Celtic enthusiasm—"she is the soul of truth and of honour."

"The vermiform appendix——" began the Professor.

"She is an angel from heaven," interrupted the other. "I fear that it is my advocacy of scientific freedom in religious thought which stands in my way with her."

"You must not truckle upon that point. You must be true to your convictions; let there be no compromise there."

"My reason is true to agnosticism, and yet I am conscious of a void—a vacuum. I had feelings at the old church at home between the scent of the incense and the roll of the organ, such as I have never experienced in the laboratory or the lecture-room."

"Sensuous—purely sensuous," said the Professor, rubbing his chin. "Vague hereditary tendencies stirred into life by the stimulation of the nasal and auditory nerves."

"Maybe so, maybe so," the younger man answered thoughtfully. "But this was not what I wished to speak to you about. Before I enter your family, your sister and you have a claim to know all that I can tell you about my career. Of my worldly prospects I have already spoken to you. There is only one point which I have omitted to mention. I am a widower."

The Professor raised his eyebrows.

"This is news indeed," said he.

"I married shortly after my arrival in Australia. Miss Thurston was her name. I met her in society. It was a most unhappy match."

Some painful emotion possessed him. His quick, expressive features quivered, and his white hands tightened upon the arms of the chair. The Professor turned away towards the window.

"You are the best judge," he remarked; "but I should not think that it was necessary to go into details."

"You have a right to know everything—you and Miss Grey. It is not a matter on which I can well speak to her direct. Poor Jinny was the best of women, but she was open to flattery, and liable to be misled by designing persons. She was untrue to me, Grey. It is a hard thing to say of the dead, but she was untrue to me. She fled to Auckland with a man whom she had known before her marriage. The brig which carried them foundered, and not a soul was saved."

"This is very painful, O'Brien," said the Professor, with a deprecatory motion of his hand. "I cannot see, however, how it affects your relation to my sister."

"I have eased my conscience," said O'Brien, rising from his chair; "I have told you all that there is to tell. I should not like the story to reach you through any lips but my own."

"You are right, O'Brien. Your action has been most honourable and considerate. But you are not to blame in the matter, save that perhaps you showed a little precipitancy in choosing a life-partner without due care and inquiry."

O'Brien drew his hand across his eyes.

"Poor girl!" he cried. "God help me, I love her still. But I must go."

"You will lunch with us?"

"No, Professor; I have my packing still to do. I have already bade Miss Grey adieu. In two months I shall see you again."

"You will probably find me a married man."

"Married!"

"Yes, I have been thinking of it."

"My dear Professor, let me congratulate you with all my heart. I had no idea. Who is the lady?"

"Mrs. O'James is her name—a widow of the same nationality as yourself. But to return to matters of importance, I should be very happy to see the proofs of your paper upon the vermiform appendix. I may be able to furnish you with material for a footnote or two."

"Your assistance will be invaluable to me," said O'Brien, with enthusiasm, and the two men parted in the hall. The Professor walked back into the dining-room, where his sister was already seated at the luncheon-table.

"I shall be married at the registrar's," he remarked; "I should strongly recommend you to do the same."

Professor Ainslie Grey was as good as his word. A fortnight's cessation of his classes gave him an opportunity which was too good to let pass. Mrs. O'James was an orphan, without relations and almost without friends in the country. There was no obstacle in the way of a speedy wedding. They were married, accordingly, in the quietest manner possible, and went off to Cambridge together, where the Professor and his charming wife were present at several academic observances, and varied the routine of their honeymoon by incursions into biological laboratories and medical libraries. Scientific friends were loud in their congratulations, not only upon Mrs. Grey's beauty, but upon the unusual quickness and intelligence she displayed in discussing physiological questions. The Professor was himself astonished at the accuracy of her information. "You have a remarkable range of knowledge for a woman, Jeannette," he remarked upon more than one occasion. He was even prepared to admit that her cerebrum might be of the normal weight.

One foggy, drizzling morning they returned to Birchespool, for the next day would reopen the session, and Professor Ainslie Grey prided himself upon having never once in his life failed to appear in his lecture-room at the very stroke of the hour. Miss Ada Grey welcomed them with a constrained cordiality, handed over the keys of office to the new mistress. Mrs. Grey pressed her warmly to remain, but she explained that she had already accepted an invitation which would engage her for some months. The same evening she departed for the south of England.

A couple of days later the maid carried a card just after breakfast into the library where the Professor sat revising his morning lecture. It announced the rearrival of Dr. James M'Murdo O'Brien. Their meeting was effusively genial on the part of the younger man, and coldly precise on that of his former teacher.

"You see there have been changes," said the Professor.

"So I heard. Miss Grey told me in her letters, and I read the notice in the British Medical Journal. So it's really married you are. How quickly and quietly you have managed it all!"

"I am constitutionally averse to anything in the nature of show or ceremony. My wife is a sensible woman—I may even go the length of saying that, for a woman, she is abnormally sensible. She quite agreed with me in the course which I have adopted."

"And your research on Vallisneria?"

"This matrimonial incident has interrupted it, but I have resumed my classes, and we shall soon be quite in harness again."

"I must see Miss Grey before I leave England. We have corresponded, and I think that all will be well. She must come out with me. I don't think I could go without her."

The Professor shook his head.

"Your nature is not so weak as you pretend," he said, "Questions of this sort are, after all, quite subordinate to the great duties of life."

O'Brien smiled.

"You would have me take out my Celtic soul and put in a Saxon one," he said. "Either my brain is too small or my heart is too big. But when may I call and pay my respects to Mrs. Grey? Will she be at home this afternoon?"

"She is at home now. Come into the morning-room. She will be glad to make your acquaintance."

They walked across the linoleum-paved hall. The Professor opened the door of the room, and walked in, followed by his friend. Mrs. Grey was sitting in a basket-chair by the window, light and fairy-like in a loose-flowing, pink morning gown. Seeing a visitor, she rose and swept towards them. The Professor heard a dull thud behind him. O'Brien had fallen back into a chair, with his hand pressed tight to his side.

"Jinny!" he gasped—"Jinny!"

Mrs. Grey stopped dead in her advance, and stared at him with a face from which every expression had been struck out, save one of astonishment and horror. Then with a sharp intaking of the breath she reeled, and would have fallen had the Professor not thrown his long, nervous arm round her.

"Try this sofa," said he.

She sank back among the cushions with the same white, cold, dead look upon her face. The Professor stood with his back to the empty fireplace and glanced from the one to the other.

"So, O'Brien," he said at last, "you have already made the acquaintance of my wife!"

"Your wife," cried his friend hoarsely. "She is no wife of yours. God help me, she is my wife."

The Professor stood rigidly upon the hearth-rug. His long, thin fingers were intertwined, and his head had sunk a little forward. His two companions had eyes only for each other.

"Jinny!" said he.

"James!"

"How could you leave me so, Jinny? How could you have the heart to do it? I thought you were dead. I mourned for your death—ay, and you have made me mourn for you living. You have withered my life."

She made no answer, but lay back among the cushions with her eyes still fixed upon him.

"Why do you not speak?"

"Because you are right, James. I have treated you cruelly—shamefully. But it is not as bad as you think."

"You fled with De Horta."

"No, I did not. At the last moment my better nature prevailed. He went alone. But I was ashamed to come back after what I had written to you. I could not face you. I took passage alone to England under a new name, and here I have lived ever since. It seemed to me that I was beginning life again. I knew that you thought I was drowned. Who could have dreamed that Fate would throw us together again! When the Professor asked me——"

She stopped and gave a gasp for breath.

"You are faint," said the Professor—"keep the head low; it aids the cerebral circulation." He flattened down the cushion. "I am sorry to leave you, O'Brien; but I have my class duties to look to. Possibly I may find you here when I return."

With a grim and rigid face he strode out of the room. Not one of the three hundred students who listened to his lecture saw any change in his manner and appearance, or could have guessed that the austere gentleman in front of them had found out at last how hard it is to rise above one's humanity. The lecture over, he performed his routine duties in the laboratory, and then drove back to his own house. He did not enter by the front door, but passed through the garden to the folding glass casement which led out of the morning-room. As he approached he heard his wife's voice and O'Brien's in loud and animated talk. He paused among the rose-bushes, uncertain whether to interrupt them or no. Nothing was further from his nature than to play the eavesdropper; but as he stood, still hesitating, words fell upon his ear which struck him rigid and motionless.

"You are still my wife, Jinny," said O'Brien; "I forgive you from the bottom of my heart. I love you, and I have never ceased to love you, though you had forgotten me."

"No, James, my heart was always in Melbourne. I have always been yours. I thought that it was better for you that I should seem to be dead."

"You must choose between us now, Jinny. If you determine to remain here, I shall not open my lips. There shall be no scandal. If, on the other hand, you come with me, it's little I care about the world's opinion. Perhaps I am as much to blame as you are. I thought too much of my work and too little of my wife."

The Professor heard the cooing, caressing laugh which he knew so well.

"I shall go with you, James," she said.

"And the Professor——?"

"The poor Professor! But he will not mind much, James; he has no heart."

"We must tell him our resolution."

"There is no need," said Professor Ainslie Grey, stepping in through the open casement. "I have overheard the latter part of your conversation. I hesitated to interrupt you before you came to a conclusion."

O'Brien stretched out his hand and took that of the woman. They stood together with the sunshine on their faces. The Professor paused at the casement with his hands behind his back and his long black shadow fell between them.

"You have come to a wise decision," said he. "Go back to Australia together, and let what has passed be blotted out of your lives."

"But you—you——" stammered O'Brien.

The Professor waved his hand.

"Never trouble about me," he said.

The woman gave a gasping cry.

"What can I do or say?" she wailed. "How could I have foreseen this? I thought my old life was dead. But it has come back again, with all its hopes and its desires. What can I say to you, Ainslie? I have brought shame and disgrace upon a worthy man. I have blasted your life. How you must hate and loathe me! I wish to God that I had never been born!"

"I neither hate nor loathe you, Jeannette," said the Professor quietly. "You are wrong in regretting your birth, for you have a worthy mission before you in aiding the life-work of a man who has shown himself capable of the highest order of scientific research. I cannot with justice blame you personally for what has occurred. How far the individual monad is to be held responsible for hereditary and engrained tendencies, is a question upon which science has not yet said her last word."

He stood with his finger-tips touching, and his body inclined as one who is gravely expounding a difficult and impersonal subject. O'Brien had stepped forward to say something, but the other's attitude and manner froze the words upon his lips. Condolence or sympathy would be an impertinence to one who could so easily merge his private griefs in broad questions of abstract philosophy.

"It is needless to prolong the situation," the Professor continued, in the same measured tones. "My brougham stands at the door. I beg that you will use it as your own. Perhaps it would be as well that you should leave the town without unnecessary delay. Your things, Jeannette, shall be forwarded."

O'Brien hesitated with a hanging head.

"I hardly dare offer you my hand," he said.

"On the contrary. I think that of the three of us you come best out of the affair. You have nothing to be ashamed of."

"Your sister—"

"I shall see that the matter is put to her in its true light. Good-bye! Let me have a copy of your recent research. Good-bye, Jeannette!"

"Good-bye!"

Their hands met, and for one short moment their eyes also. It was only a glance, but for the first and last time the woman's intuition cast a light for itself into the dark places of a strong man's soul. She gave a little gasp, and her other hand rested for an instant, as white and as light as thistle-down, upon his shoulder.

"James, James!" she cried. "Don't you see that he is stricken to the heart?"

He turned her quietly away from him.

"I am not an emotional man," he said. "I have my duties—my research on Vallisneria. The brougham is there. Your cloak is in the hall. Tell John where you wish to be driven. He will faring you anything you need. Now go."

His last two words were so sudden, so volcanic, in such contrast to his measured voice and mask-like face, that they swept the two away from him. He closed the door behind them and paced slowly up and down the room. Then he passed into the library and looked out over the wire blind. The carriage was rolling away. He caught a last glimpse of the woman who had been his wife. He saw the feminine droop of her head, and the curve of her beautiful throat.

Under some foolish, aimless impulse, he took a few quick steps towards the door. Then he turned, and, throwing himself into his study chair, he plunged back into his work.

There was little scandal about this singular domestic incident. The Professor had few personal friends, and seldom went into society. His marriage had been so quiet that most of his colleagues had never ceased to regard him as a bachelor. Mrs. Esdaile and a few others might talk, but their field for gossip was limited, for they could only guess vaguely at the cause of this sudden separation.

The Professor was as punctual as ever at his classes, and as zealous in directing the laboratory work of those who studied under him. His own private researches were pushed on with feverish energy. It was no uncommon thing for his servants, when they came down of a morning, to hear the shrill scratchings of his tireless pen, or to meet him on the staircase as he ascended, grey and silent, to his room. In vain his friends assured him that such a life must undermine his health. He lengthened his hours until day and night were one long, ceaseless task.

Gradually under this discipline a change came over his appearance. His features, always inclined to gauntness, became even sharper and more pronounced. There were deep lines about his temples and across his brow. His cheek was sunken and his complexion bloodless. His knees gave under him when he walked; and once when passing out of his lecture-room he fell and had to be assisted to his carriage.

This was just before the end of the session; and soon after the holidays commenced, the professors who still remained in Birchespool were shocked to hear that their brother of the chair of physiology had sunk so low that no hopes could be entertained of his recovery. Two eminent physicians had consulted over his case without being able to give a name to the affection from which he suffered. A steadily decreasing vitality appeared to be the only symptom—a bodily weakness which left the mind unclouded. He was much interested himself in his own case, and made notes of his subjective sensations as an aid to diagnosis. Of his approaching end he spoke in his usual unemotional and somewhat pedantic fashion. "It is the assertion," he said, "of the liberty of the individual cell as opposed to the cell commune. It is the dissolution of a co-operative society. The process is one of great interest."

And so one grey morning his co-operative society dissolved. Very quietly and softly he sank into his eternal sleep. His two physicians felt some slight embarrassment when called upon to fill in his certificate.

"It is difficult to give it a name," said one.

"Very," said the other.

"If he were not such an unemotional man, I should have said that he had died from some sudden nervous shock—from, in fact, what the vulgar would call a broken heart."

"I don't think poor Grey was that sort of a man at all."

"Let us call it cardiac, anyhow," said the other physician.

So they did so.

VIII

BEHIND THE TIMES

My first interview with Dr. James Winter was under dramatic circumstances. It occurred at two in the morning in the bedroom of an old country house. I kicked him twice on the white waistcoat and knocked off his gold spectacles, while he, with the aid of a female accomplice, stifled my angry cries in a flannel petticoat and thrust me into a warm bath. I am told that one of my parents, who happened to be present, remarked in a whisper that there was nothing the matter with my lungs. I cannot recall how Dr. Winter looked at the time for I had other things to think of, but his description of my own appearance is far from flattering. A fluffy head, a body like a trussed goose, very bandy legs, and feet with the soles turned inwards—those are the main items which he can remember.

From this time onwards the epochs of my life were the periodical assaults which Dr. Winter made upon me. He vaccinated me, he cut me for an abscess, he blistered me for mumps. It was a world of peace, and he the one dark cloud that threatened. But at last there came a time of real illness—a time when I lay for months together inside my wicker-work basket bed, and then it was that I learned that that hard face could relax, that those country-made, creaking boots could steal very gently to a bedside, and that that rough voice could thin into a whisper when it spoke to a sick child.

And now the child is himself a medical man, and yet Dr. Winter is the same as ever. I can see no change since first I can remember him, save that perhaps the brindled hair is a trifle whiter, and the huge shoulders a little more bowed. He is a very tall man, though he loses a couple of inches from his stoop. That big back of his has curved itself over sick beds until it has set in that shape. His face is of a walnut brown, and tells of long winter drives over bleak country roads with the wind and the rain in his teeth. It looks smooth at a little distance, but as you approach him you see that it is shot with innumerable fine wrinkles, like a last year's apple. They are hardly to be seen when he is in repose, but when he laughs his face breaks like a starred glass, and you realise then that, though he looks old, he must be older than he looks.

How old that is I could never discover. I have often tried to find out, and have struck his stream as high up as George the Fourth and even of the Regency, but without ever getting quite to the source. His mind must have been open to impressions very early, but it must also have closed early, for the politics of the day have little interest for him, while he is fiercely excited about questions which are entirely prehistoric. He shakes his head when he speaks of the first Reform Bill and expresses grave doubts as to its wisdom, and I have heard him, when he was warmed by a glass of wine, say bitter things about Robert Peel and his abandoning of the Corn Laws. The death of that statesman brought the history of England to a definite close, and Dr. Winter refers to everything which had happened since then as to an insignificant anti-climax.

But it was only when I had myself become a medical man that I was able to appreciate how entirely he is a survival of a past generation.

He had learned his medicine under that obsolete and forgotten system by which a youth was apprenticed to a surgeon, in the days when the study of anatomy was often approached through a violated grave. His views upon his own profession are even more reactionary than his politics. Fifty years have brought him little and deprived him of less. Vaccination was well within the teaching of his youth, though I think he has a secret preference for inoculation. Bleeding he would practise freely but for public opinion. Chloroform he regards as a dangerous innovation, and he always clicks with his tongue when it is mentioned. He has even been known to say vain things about Laennec, and to refer to the stethoscope as "a newfangled French toy." He carries one in his hat out of deference to the expectations of his patients; but he is very hard of hearing, so that it makes little difference whether he uses it or not.

He always reads, as a duty, his weekly medical paper, so that he has a general idea as to the advance of modern science. He persists in looking upon it, however, as a huge and rather ludicrous experiment. The germ theory of disease set him chuckling for a long time, and his favourite joke in the sick-room was to say, "Shut the door, or the germs will be getting in." As to the Darwinian theory, it struck him as being the crowning joke of the century. "The children in the nursery and the ancestors in the stable," he would cry, and laugh the tears out of his eyes.

He is so very much behind the day that occasionally, as things move round in their usual circle, he finds himself, to his own bewilderment, in the front of the fashion. Dietetic treatment, for example, had been much in vogue in his youth, and he has more practical knowledge of it than any one whom I have met. Massage, too, was familiar to him when it was new to our generation. He had been trained also at a time when instruments were in a rudimentary state and when men learned to trust more to their own fingers. He has a model surgical hand, muscular in the palm, tapering in the fingers, "with an eye at the end of each." I shall not easily forget how Dr. Patterson and I cut Sir John Sirwell, the County Member, and were unable to find the stone. It was a horrible moment. Both our careers were at stake. And then it was that Dr. Winter, whom we had asked out of courtesy to be present, introduced into the wound a finger which seemed to our excited senses to be about nine inches long, and hooked out the stone at the end of it.

"It's always well to bring one in your waistcoat pocket," said he with a chuckle, "but I suppose you youngsters are above all that."

We made him President of our Branch of the British Medical Association, but he resigned after the first meeting. "The young men are too much for me," he said. "I don't understand what they are talking about." Yet his patients do very well. He has the healing touch—that magnetic thing which defies explanation or analysis, but which is a very evident fact none the less. His mere presence leaves the patient with more hopefulness and vitality. The sight of disease affects him as dust does a careful housewife. It makes him angry and impatient. "Tut, tut, this will never do!" he cries, as he takes over a new case. He would shoo death out of the room as though he were an intrusive hen. But when the intruder refuses to be dislodged, when the blood moves more slowly and the eyes grow dimmer, then it is that Dr. Winter is of more avail than all the drugs in his surgery. Dying folk cling to his hand as if the presence of his bulk and vigour gives them more courage to face the change; and that kindly, wind-beaten face has been the last earthly impression which many a sufferer has carried into the unknown.

When Dr. Patterson and I, both of us young, energetic, and up-to-date, settled in the district, we were most cordially received by the old doctor, who would have been only too happy to be relieved of some of his patients. The patients themselves, however, followed their own inclinations, which is a reprehensible way that patients have, so that we remained neglected with our modern instruments and our latest alkaloids, while he was serving out senna and calomel to all the country-side. We both of us loved the old fellow, but at the same time, in the privacy of our own intimate conversations, we could not help commenting upon this deplorable lack of judgment.

"It is all very well for the poorer people," said Patterson, "but after all the educated classes have a right to expect that their medical man will know the difference between a mitral murmur and a bronchitic rale. It's the judicial frame of mind, not the sympathetic, which is the essential one."

I thoroughly agreed with Patterson in what he said. It happened, however, that very shortly afterwards the epidemic of influenza broke out, and we were all worked to death. One morning I met Patterson on my round, and found him looking rather pale and fagged out. He made the same remark about me. I was in fact feeling far from well, and I lay upon the sofa all afternoon with a splitting headache and pains in every joint. As evening closed in I could no longer disguise the fact that the scourge was upon me, and I felt that I should have medical advice without delay. It was of Patterson naturally that I thought, but somehow the idea of him had suddenly become repugnant to me. I thought of his cold, critical attitude, of his endless questions, of his tests and his tappings. I wanted something more soothing—something more genial.

"Mrs. Hudson," said I to my housekeeper, "would you kindly run along to old Dr. Winter and tell him that I should be obliged to him if he would step round."

She was back with an answer presently.

"Dr. Winter will come round in an hour or so, sir, but he has just been called in to attend Dr. Patterson."

IX

HIS FIRST OPERATION

It was the first day of a winter session, and the third year's man was walking with the first year's man. Twelve o'clock was just booming out from the Tron Church.

"Let me see," said the third year's man, "you have never seen an operation?"

"Never."

"Then this way, please. This is Rutherford's historic bar. A glass of sherry, please, for this gentleman. You are rather sensitive, are you not?"

"My nerves are not very strong, I am afraid."

"Hum! Another glass of sherry for this gentleman. We are going to an operation now, you know."

The novice squared his shoulders and made a gallant attempt to look unconcerned.

"Nothing very bad—eh?"

"Well, yes—pretty bad."

"An—an amputation?"

"No, it's a bigger affair than that."

"I think—I think they must be expecting me at home."

"There's no sense in funking. If you don't go to-day you must to-morrow. Better get it over at once. Feel pretty fit?"

"Oh, yes, all right."

The smile was not a success.

"One more glass of sherry, then. Now come on or we shall be late. I want you to be well in front."

"Surely that is not necessary."

"Oh, it is far better. What a drove of students! There are plenty of new men among them. You can tell them easily enough, can't you? If they were going down to be operated upon themselves they could not look whiter."

"I don't think I should look as white."

"Well, I was just the same myself. But the feeling soon wears off. You see a fellow with a face like plaster, and before the week is out he is eating his lunch in the dissecting rooms. I'll tell you all about the case when we get to the theatre."

The students were pouring down the sloping street which led to the infirmary—each with his little sheaf of note-books in his hand. There were pale, frightened lads, fresh from the High Schools, and callous old chronics, whose generation had passed on and left them. They swept in an unbroken, tumultuous stream from the University gate to the hospital. The figures and gait of the men were young, but there was little youth in most of their faces. Some looked as if they ate too little—a few as if they drank too much. Tall and short, tweed coated and black, round-shouldered, bespectacled and slim, they crowded with clatter of feet and rattle of sticks through the hospital gate. Now and again they thickened into two lines as the carriage of a surgeon of the staff rolled over the cobblestones between.

"There's going to be a crowd at Archer's," whispered the senior man with suppressed excitement. "It is grand to see him at work. I've seen him jab all round the aorta until it made me jumpy to watch him. This way, and mind the whitewash."

They passed under an archway and down a long, stone-flagged corridor with drab-coloured doors on either side, each marked with a number. Some of them were ajar, and the novice glanced into them with tingling nerves. He was reassured to catch a glimpse of cheery fires, lines of white-counterpaned beds and a profusion of coloured texts upon the wall. The corridor opened upon a small hall with a fringe of poorly-clad people seated all round upon benches. A young man with a pair of scissors stuck, like a flower, in his button-hole, and a note-book in his hand, was passing from one to the other, whispering and writing.

"Anything good?" asked the third year's man.

"You should have been here yesterday," said the out-patient clerk, glancing up. "We had a regular field day. A popliteal aneurism, a Colles' fracture, a spina bifida, a tropical abscess, and an elephantiasis. How's that for a single haul?"

"I'm sorry I missed it. But they'll come again, I suppose. What's up with the old gentleman?"

A broken workman was sitting in the shadow, rocking himself slowly to and fro and groaning. A woman beside him was trying to console him, patting his shoulder with a hand which was spotted over with curious little white blisters.

"It's a fine carbuncle," said the clerk, with the air of a connoisseur who describes his orchids to one who can appreciate them. "It's on his back, and the passage is draughty, so we must not look at it, must we, daddy? Pemphigus," he added carelessly, pointing to the woman's disfigured hands. "Would you care to stop and take out a metacarpal?"

"No, thank you, we are due at Archer's. Come on;" and they rejoined the throng, which was hurrying to the theatre of the famous surgeon.

The tiers of horseshoe benches, rising from the floor to the ceiling, were already packed, and the novice as he entered saw vague, curving lines of faces in front of him, and heard the deep buzz of a hundred voices and sounds of laughter from somewhere up above him. His companion spied an opening on the second bench, and they both squeezed into it.

"This is grand," the senior man whispered; "you'll have a rare view of it all."

Only a single row of heads intervened between them and the operating table. It was of unpainted deal, plain, strong and scrupulously clean. A sheet of brown waterproofing covered half of it, and beneath stood a large tin tray full of sawdust. On the farther side, in front of the window, there was a board which was strewed with glittering instruments, forceps, tenacula, saws, canulas, and trocars. A line of knives, with long, thin, delicate blades, lay at one side. Two young men lounged in front of this; one threading needles, the other doing something to a brass coffee-pot-like thing which hissed out puffs of steam.

"That's Peterson," whispered the senior. "The big, bald man in the front row. He's the skin-grafting man, you know. And that's Anthony Browne, who took a larynx out successfully last winter. And there's Murphy the pathologist, and Stoddart the eye man. You'll come to know them all soon."

"Who are the two men at the table?"

"Nobody—dressers. One has charge of the instruments and the other of the puffing Billy. It's Lister's antiseptic spray, you know, and Archer's one of the carbolic acid men. Hayes is the leader of the cleanliness-and-cold-water school, and they all hate each other like poison."

A flutter of interest passed through the closely-packed benches as a woman in petticoat and bodice was led in by two nurses. A red woollen shawl was draped over her head and round her neck. The face which looked out from it was that of a woman in the prime of her years, but drawn with suffering and of a peculiar bees-wax tint. Her head drooped as she walked, and one of the nurses, with her arm round her waist, was whispering consolation in her ear. She gave a quick side glance at the instrument table as she passed, but the nurses turned her away from it.

"What ails her?" asked the novice.

"Cancer of the parotid. It's the devil of a case, extends right away back behind the carotids. There's hardly a man but Archer would dare to follow it. Ah, here he is himself."

As he spoke, a small, brisk, iron-grey man came striding into the room, rubbing his hands together as he walked. He had a clean-shaven face of the Naval officer type, with large, bright eyes, and a firm, straight mouth. Behind him came his big house surgeon with his gleaming pince-nez and a trail of dressers, who grouped themselves into the corners of the room.

"Gentlemen," cried the surgeon in a voice as hard and brisk as his manner. "We have here an interesting case of tumour of the parotid, originally cartilaginous but now assuming malignant characteristics, and therefore requiring excision. On to the table, nurse! Thank you! Chloroform, clerk! Thank you! You can take the shawl off, nurse."

The woman lay back upon the waterproofed pillow and her murderous tumour lay revealed. In itself it was a pretty thing, ivory white with a mesh of blue veins, and curving gently from jaw to chest. But the lean, yellow face, and the stringy throat were in horrible contrast with the plumpness and sleekness of this monstrous growth. The surgeon placed a hand on each side of it and pressed it slowly backwards and forwards.

"Adherent at one place, gentlemen," he cried. "The growth involves the carotids and jugulars, and passes behind the ramus of the jaw, whither we must be prepared to follow it. It is impossible to say how deep our dissection may carry us. Carbolic tray, thank you! Dressings of carbolic gauze, if you please! Push the chloroform, Mr. Johnson. Have the small saw ready in case it is necessary to remove the jaw."

The patient was moaning gently under the towel which had been placed over her face. She tried to raise her arms and to draw up her knees but two dressers restrained her. The heavy air was full of the penetrating smells of carbolic acid and of chloroform. A muffled cry came from under the towel and then a snatch of a song, sung in a high, quavering, monotonous voice.

"He says, says he,

If you fly with me

You'll be mistress of the ice-cream van;

You'll be mistress of the——"

It mumbled off into a drone and stopped. The surgeon came across, still rubbing his hands, and spoke to an elderly man in front of the novice.

"Narrow squeak for the Government," he said.

"Oh, ten is enough."

"They won't have ten long. They'd do better to resign before they are driven to it."

"Oh, I should fight it out."

"What's the use. They can't get past the committee, even if they get a vote in the House. I was talking to——"

"Patient's ready, sir," said the dresser.

"Talking to M'Donald—but I'll tell you about it presently." He walked back to the patient, who was breathing in long, heavy gasps. "I propose," said he, passing his hands over the tumour in an almost caressing fashion, "to make a free incision over the posterior border and to take another forward at right angles to the lower end of it. Might I trouble you for a medium knife, Mr. Johnson?"

The novice, with eyes which were dilating with horror, saw the surgeon pick up the long, gleaming knife, dip it into a tin basin and balance it in his fingers as an artist might his brush. Then he saw him pinch up the skin above the tumour with his left hand. At the sight, his nerves, which had already been tried once or twice that day, gave way utterly. His head swam round and he felt that in another instant he might faint. He dared not look at the patient. He dug his thumbs into his ears lest some scream should come to haunt him, and he fixed his eyes rigidly upon the wooden ledge in front of him. One glance, one cry, would, he knew, break down the shred of self-possession which he still retained. He tried to think of cricket, of green fields and rippling water, of his sisters at home—of anything rather than of what was going on so near him.

And yet, somehow, even with his ears stopped up, sounds seemed to penetrate to him and to carry their own tale. He heard, or thought that he heard, the long hissing of the carbolic engine. Then he was conscious of some movement among the dressers. Were there groans too breaking in upon him, and some other sound, some fluid sound, which was more dreadfully suggestive still? His mind would keep building up every step of the operation, and fancy made it more ghastly than fact could have been. His nerves tingled and quivered. Minute by minute the giddiness grew more marked, the numb, sickly feeling at his heart more distressing. And then suddenly, with a groan, his head pitching forward and his brow cracking sharply upon the narrow, wooden shelf in front of him, he lay in a dead faint.

When he came to himself he was lying in the empty theatre with his collar and shirt undone. The third year's man was dabbing a wet sponge over his face, and a couple of grinning dressers were looking on.

"All right," cried the novice, sitting up and rubbing his eyes; "I'm sorry to have made an ass of myself."

"Well, so I should think," said his companion. "What on earth did you faint about?"

"I couldn't help it. It was that operation."

"What operation?"

"Why, that cancer."

There was a pause, and then the three students burst out laughing.

"Why, you juggins," cried the senior man, "there never was an operation at all. They found the patient didn't stand the chloroform well, and so the whole thing was off. Archer has been giving us one of his racy lectures, and you fainted just in the middle of his favourite story."

X

THE THIRD GENERATION

Scudamore Lane, sloping down riverwards from just behind the Monument, lies at night in the shadow of two black and monstrous walls which loom high above the glimmer of the scattered gas-lamps. The footpaths are narrow, and the causeway is paved with rounded cobblestones so that the endless drays roar along it like so many breaking waves. A few old-fashioned houses lie scattered among the business premises, and in one of these—half-way down on the left-hand side—Dr. Horace Selby conducts his large practice. It is a singular street for so big a man, but a specialist who has a European reputation can afford to live where he likes. In his particular branch, too, patients do not always consider seclusion to be a disadvantage.

It was only ten o'clock. The dull roar of the traffic which converged all day upon London Bridge had died away now to a mere confused murmur. It was raining heavily, and the gas shone dimly through the streaked and dripping glass, throwing little yellow circles upon the glistening cobblestones. The air was full of the sounds of rain, the thin swish of its fall, the heavier drip from the eaves, and the swirl and gurgle down the two steep gutters and through the sewer grating. There was only one figure in the whole length of Scudamore Lane. It was that of a man, and it stood outside the door of Dr. Horace Selby.

He had just rung and was waiting for an answer. The fanlight beat full upon the gleaming shoulders of his waterproof and upon his upturned features. It was a wan, sensitive, clear-cut face, with some subtle, nameless peculiarity in its expression—something of the startled horse in the white-rimmed eye, something, too, of the helpless child in the drawn cheek and the weakening of the lower lip. The man-servant knew the stranger as a patient at a bare glance at those frightened eyes. Such a look had been seen at that door before.

"Is the doctor in?"

The man hesitated.

"He has had a few friends to dinner, sir. He does not like to be disturbed outside his usual hours, sir."

"Tell him that I must see him. Tell him that it is of the very first importance. Here is my card." He fumbled with his trembling fingers in trying to draw one from the case. "Sir Francis Norton is the name. Tell him that Sir Francis Norton of Deane Park must see him at once."

"Yes, sir." The butler closed his fingers upon the card and the half-sovereign which accompanied it. "Better hang your coat up here in the hall. It is very wet. Now, if you will wait here in the consulting-room I have no doubt that I shall be able to send the doctor in to you."

It was a large and lofty room in which the young baronet found himself. The carpet was so soft and thick that his feet made no sound as he walked across it. The two gas-jets were turned only half-way up, and the dim light with the faint aromatic smell which filled the air had a vaguely religious suggestion. He sat down in a shining leather arm-chair by the smouldering fire and looked gloomily about him. Two sides of the room were taken up with books, fat and sombre, with broad gold lettering upon their backs. Beside him was the high, old-fashioned mantelpiece of white marble, the top of it strewed with cotton wadding and bandages, graduated measures and little bottles. There was one with a broad neck, just above him, containing bluestone, and another narrower one with what looked like the ruins of a broken pipe stem, and "Caustic" outside upon a red label. Thermometers, hypodermic syringes, bistouries and spatulas were scattered thickly about, both on the mantelpiece and on the central table on either side of the sloping desk. On the same table to the right stood copies of the five books which Dr. Horace Selby had written upon the subject with which his name is peculiarly associated, while on the left, on the top of a red medical directory, lay a huge glass model of a human eye, the size of a turnip, which opened down the centre to expose the lens and double chamber within.

Sir Francis Norton had never been remarkable for his powers of observation, and yet he found himself watching these trifles with the keenest attention. Even the corrosion of the cork of an acid bottle caught his eye and he wondered that the doctor did not use glass stoppers. Tiny scratches where the light glinted off from the table, little stains upon the leather of the desk, chemical formulæ scribbled upon the labels of some of the phials—nothing was too slight to arrest his attention. And his sense of hearing was equally alert. The heavy ticking of the solemn black clock above the fireplace struck quite painfully upon his ears. Yet, in spite of it, and in spite also of the thick, old-fashioned, wooden partition walls, he could hear the voices of men talking in the next room and could even catch scraps of their conversation. "Second hand was bound to take it." "Why, you drew the last of them yourself." "How could I play the queen when I knew the ace was against me?" The phrases came in little spurts, falling back into the dull murmur of conversation. And then suddenly he heard a creaking of a door, and a step in the hall, and knew with a tingling mixture of impatience and horror that the crisis of his life was at hand.

Dr. Horace Selby was a large, portly man, with an imposing presence. His nose and chin were bold and pronounced, yet his features were puffy—a combination which would blend more freely with the wig and cravat of the early Georges, than with the close-cropped hair and black frockcoat of the end of the nineteenth century. He was clean shaven, for his mouth was too good to cover, large, flexible and sensitive, with a kindly human softening at either corner, which, with his brown, sympathetic eyes, had drawn out many a shame-struck sinner's secret. Two masterful little bushy side whiskers bristled out from under his ears, spindling away upwards to merge in the thick curves of his brindled hair. To his patients there was something reassuring in the mere bulk and dignity of the man. A high and easy bearing in medicine, as in war, bears with it a hint of victories in the past, and a promise of others to come. Dr.

Horace Selby's face was a consolation, and so, too, were the large, white, soothing hands, one of which he held out to his visitor.

"I am sorry to have kept you waiting. It is a conflict of duties, you perceive. A host to his guests and an adviser to his patient. But now I am entirely at your disposal, Sir Francis. But, dear me, you are very cold."

"Yes, I am cold."

"And you are trembling all over. Tut, tut, this will never do. This miserable night has chilled you. Perhaps some little stimulant——"

"No, thank you. I would really rather not. And it is not the night which has chilled me. I am frightened, doctor."

The doctor half turned in his chair and patted the arch of the young man's knee as he might the neck of a restless horse.

"What, then?" he asked, looking over his shoulder at the pale face with the startled eyes.

Twice the young man parted his lips. Then he stooped with a sudden gesture and turning up the right leg of his trousers he pulled down his sock and thrust forward his shin. The doctor made a clicking noise with his tongue as he glanced at it.

"Both legs?"

"No, only one."

"Suddenly?"

"This morning."

"Hum!" The doctor pouted his lips, and drew his finger and thumb down the line of his chin. "Can you account for it?" he said briskly.

"No."

A trace of sternness came into the large, brown eyes.

"I need not point out to you that unless the most absolute frankness——"

The patient sprang from his chair.

"So help me God, doctor," he cried, "I have nothing in my life with which to reproach myself. Do you think that I would be such a fool as to come here and tell you lies? Once for all, I have nothing to regret."

He was a pitiful, half-tragic, and half-grotesque figure as he stood with one trouser leg rolled to his knee, and that ever-present horror still lurking in his eyes. A burst of merriment came from the card players in the next room and the two looked at each other in silence.

"Sit down!" said the doctor abruptly. "Your assurance is quite sufficient." He stooped and ran his finger down the line of the young man's shin, raising it at one point. "Hum! Serpiginous!" he murmured, shaking his head; "any other symptoms?"

"My eyes have been a little weak."

"Let me see your teeth!" He glanced at them, and again made the gentle clicking sound of sympathy and disapprobation.

"Now the eye!" He lit a lamp at the patient's elbow, and holding a small crystal lens to concentrate the light, he threw it obliquely upon the patient's eye. As he did so a glow of pleasure came over his large, expressive face, a flush of such enthusiasm as the botanist feels when he packs the rare plant into his tin knapsack, or the astronomer when the long-sought comet first swims into the field of his telescope.

"This is very typical—very typical indeed," he murmured, turning to his desk and jotting down a few memoranda upon a sheet of paper. "Curiously enough I am writing a monograph upon the subject. It is singular that you should have been able to furnish so well marked a case."

He had so forgotten the patient in his symptom that he had assumed an almost congratulatory air towards its possessor. He reverted to human sympathy again as his patient asked for particulars.

"My dear sir, there is no occasion for us to go into strictly professional details together," said he soothingly. "If, for example, I were to say that you have interstitial keratitis, how would you be the wiser? There are indications of a strumous diathesis. In broad terms I may say that you have a constitutional and hereditary taint."

The young baronet sank back in his chair and his chin fell forward upon his chest. The doctor sprang to a side table and poured out a half glass of liqueur brandy which he held to his patient's lips. A little fleck of colour came into his cheeks as he drank it down.

"Perhaps I spoke a little abruptly," said the doctor. "But you must have known the nature of your complaint, why otherwise should you have come to me?"

"God help me, I suspected it—but only to-day when my leg grew bad. My father had a leg like this."

"It was from him, then?"

"No, from my grandfather. You have heard of Sir Rupert Norton, the great Corinthian?"

The doctor was a man of wide reading with a retentive memory. The name brought back to him instantly the remembrance of the sinister reputation of its owner—a notorious buck of the thirties, who had gambled and duelled and steeped himself in drink and debauchery until even the vile set with whom he consorted had shrunk away from him in horror, and left him to a sinister old age with the barmaid wife whom in some drunken frolic he had espoused. As he looked at the young man still leaning back in the leather chair, there seemed for the instant to flicker up behind him some vague presentiment of that foul old dandy with his dangling seals, many-wreathed scarf, and dark, satyric face. What was he now? An armful of bones in a mouldy box. But his deeds—they were living and rotting the blood in the veins of an innocent man.

"I see that you have heard of him," said the young baronet. "He died horribly, I have been told, but not more horribly than he had lived. My father was his only son. He was a studious, man, fond of books and canaries and the country. But his innocent life did not save him."

"His symptoms were cutaneous, I understand."

"He wore gloves in the house. That was the first thing I can remember. And then it was his throat, and then his legs. He used to ask me so often about my own health, and I thought him so fussy, for how could I tell what the meaning of it was? He was always watching me—always with a sidelong eye fixed upon me. Now at last I know what he was watching for."

"Had you brothers or sisters?"

"None, thank God!"

"Well, well, it is a sad case, and very typical of many which come in my way. You are no lonely sufferer, Sir Francis. There are many thousands who bear the same cross as you do."

"But where's the justice of it, doctor?" cried the young man, springing from the chair and pacing up and down the consulting-room. "If I were heir to my grandfather's sins as well as to their results I could understand it, but I am of my father's type; I love all that is gentle and beautiful, music and poetry and art. The coarse and animal is abhorrent to me. Ask any of my friends and they would tell you that. And now that this vile, loathsome thing—Ach, I am polluted to the marrow, soaked in abomination! And why? Haven't I a right to ask why? Did I do it? Was it my fault? Could I help being born? And look at me now, blighted and blasted, just as life was at its sweetest! Talk about the sins of the father! How about the sins of the Creator!" He shook his two clenched hands in the air, the poor, impotent atom with his pinpoint of brain caught in the whirl of the infinite.

The doctor rose and placing his hands upon his shoulders he pressed him back into his chair again.

"There, there, my dear lad," said he. "You must not excite yourself! You are trembling all over. Your nerves cannot stand it. We must take these great questions upon trust. What are we after all? Half evolved creatures in a transition stage; nearer, perhaps, to the medusa on the one side than to perfected humanity on the other. With half a complete brain we can't expect to understand the whole of a complete fact, can we, now? It is all very dim and dark, no doubt, but I think Pope's famous couplet sums the whole matter up, and from my heart, after fifty years of varied experience, I can say that——"

But the young baronet gave a cry of impatience and disgust.

"Words, words, words! You can sit comfortably there in your chair and say them—and think them too, no doubt. You've had your life. But I've never had mine. You've healthy blood in your veins. Mine is putrid. And yet I am as innocent as you. What would words do for you if you were in this chair and I in that? Ah, it's such a mockery and a make-belief. Don't think me rude, though, doctor. I don't mean to be that. I only say that it is impossible for you or any man to realise it. But I've a question to ask you, doctor. It's one on which my whole life must depend."

He writhed his fingers together in an agony of apprehension.

"Speak out, my dear sir. I have every sympathy with you."

"Do you think—do you think the poison has spent itself on me? Do you think if I had children that they would suffer?"

"I can only give one answer to that. 'The third and fourth generation,' says the trite old text. You may in time eliminate it from your system, but many years must pass before you can think of marriage."

"I am to be married on Tuesday," whispered the patient.

It was Dr. Horace Selby's turn to be thrilled with horror. There were not many situations which would yield such a sensation to his well-seasoned nerves. He sat in silence while the babble of the card-table broke in again upon them. "We had a double ruff if you had returned a heart." "I was bound to clear the trumps." They were hot and angry about it.

"How could you?" cried the doctor severely. "It was criminal."

"You forget that I have only learned how I stand to-day." He put his two hands to his temples and pressed them convulsively. "You are a man of the world, Doctor Selby. You have seen or heard of such things before. Give me some advice. I'm in your hands. It is all so sudden and horrible, and I don't think I am strong enough to bear it."

The doctor's heavy brows thickened into two straight lines and he bit his nails in perplexity.

"The marriage must not take place."

"Then what am I to do?"

"At all costs it must not take place."

"And I must give her up?"

"There can be no question about that!"

The young man took out a pocket-book and drew from it a small photograph, holding it out towards the doctor. The firm face softened as he looked at it.

"It is very hard on you, no doubt. I can appreciate it more now that I have seen that. But there is no alternative at all. You must give up all thought of it."

"But this is madness, doctor—madness, I tell you. No, I won't raise my voice! I forgot myself! But realise it, man! I am to be married on Tuesday—this coming Tuesday, you know. And all the world knows it. How can I put such a public affront upon her? It would be monstrous."

"None the less it must be done. My dear sir, there is no way out of it."

"You would have me simply write brutally and break the engagement at this last moment without a reason? I tell you I couldn't do it."

"I had a patient once who found himself in a somewhat similar situation some years ago," said the doctor thoughtfully. "His device was a singular one. He deliberately committed a penal offence and so compelled the young lady's people to withdraw their consent to the marriage."

The young baronet shook his head.

"My personal honour is as yet unstained," said he. "I have little else left, but that at least I will preserve."

"Well, well, it's a nice dilemma and the choice lies with you."

"Have you no other suggestion?"

"You don't happen to have property in Australia?"

"None."

"But you have capital?"

"Yes."

"Then you could buy some—to-morrow morning, for example. A thousand mining shares would do. Then you might write to say that urgent business affairs have compelled you to start at an hour's notice to inspect your property. That would give you six months at any rate."

"Well, that would be possible—yes, certainly it would be possible. But think of her position—the house full of wedding presents— guests coming from a distance. It is awful. And you say there is no alternative."

The doctor shrugged his shoulders.

"Well, then, I might write it now, and start to-morrow—eh? Perhaps you would let me use your desk. Thank you! I am so sorry to keep you from your guests so long. But I won't be a moment now." He wrote an abrupt note of a few lines. Then, with a sudden impulse, he tore it to shreds and flung it into the fireplace. "No, I can't sit down and tell her a lie, doctor," said he rising. "We must find some other way out of this. I will think it over, and let you know my decision. You must allow me to double your fee as I have taken such an unconscionable time. Now, good-bye, and thank you a thousand times for your sympathy and advice."

"Why, dear me, you haven't even got your prescription yet. This is the mixture, and I should recommend one of these powders every morning and the chemist will put all directions upon the ointment box. You are placed in a cruel situation, but I trust that these may be but passing clouds. When may I hope to hear from you again?"

"To-morrow morning."

"Very good. How the rain is splashing in the street. You have your waterproof there. You will need it. Good-bye, then, until to-morrow."

He opened the door. A gust of cold, damp air swept into the hall. And yet the doctor stood for a minute or more watching the lonely figure which passed slowly through the yellow splotches of the gas-lamps and into the broad bars of darkness between. It was but his own shadow which trailed up the wall as he passed the lights, and yet it looked to the doctor's eye as though some huge and sombre figure walked by a mannikin's side, and led him silently up the lonely street.

Doctor Horace Selby heard again of his patient next morning and rather earlier than he had expected. A paragraph in the Daily News caused him to push away his breakfast untasted, and turned him sick and faint while he read it. "A Deplorable Accident" it was headed, and it ran in this way:—

"A fatal accident of a peculiarly painful character is reported from King William Street. About eleven o'clock last night a young man was observed, while endeavouring to get out of the way of a hansom, to slip and fall under the wheels of a heavy two-horse dray. On being picked up, his injuries were found to be of a most shocking character, and he expired while being conveyed to the hospital. An examination of his pocket-book and card-case shows beyond any question that the deceased is none other than Sir Francis Norton of Deane Park, who has only within the last year come into the baronetcy. The accident is made the more deplorable as the deceased, who was only just of age, was on the eve of being married to a young lady belonging to one of the oldest families in the south. With his wealth and his talents the ball of fortune was at his feet, and his many friends will be deeply grieved to know that his promising career has been cut short in so sudden and tragic a fashion."

XI

THE CURSE OF EVE

Robert Johnson was an essentially commonplace man, with no feature to distinguish him from a million others. He was pale of face, ordinary in looks, neutral in opinions, thirty years of age, and a married man. By trade he was a gentleman's outfitter in the New North Road, and the competition of business squeezed out of him the little character that was left. In his hope of conciliating customers he had become cringing and pliable, until working ever In the same routine from day to day he seemed to have sunk into a soulless machine rather than a man. No great question had ever stirred him. At the end of this smug century, self-contained in his own narrow circle, it seemed impossible that any of the mighty, primitive passions of mankind could ever reach him. Yet birth, and lust, and illness, and death are changeless things, and when one of these harsh facts springs out upon a man at some sudden turn of the path of life, it dashes off for the moment his mask of civilisation and gives a glimpse of the stranger and stronger face below.

Johnson's wife was a quiet little woman, with brown hair and gentle ways. His affection for her was the one positive trait in his character. Together they would lay out the shop window every Monday morning, the spotless shirts in their green cardboard boxes below, the neckties above hung in rows over the brass rails, the cheap studs glistening from the white cards at either side, while in the background were the rows of cloth caps and the bank of boxes in which the more valuable hats were screened from the sunlight. She kept the books and sent out the bills. No one but she knew the joys and sorrows which crept into his small life. She had shared his exultation when the gentleman who was going to India had bought ten dozen shirts and an incredible number of collars, and she had been stricken as he when, after the goods had gone, the bill was returned from the hotel address with the intimation that no such person had lodged there. For five years they had worked, building up the business, thrown together all the more closely because their marriage had been a childless one. Now, however, there were signs that a change was at hand, and that speedily. She was unable to come downstairs, and her mother, Mrs. Peyton, came over from Camberwell to nurse her and to welcome her grandchild.

Little qualms of anxiety came over Johnson as his wife's time approached. However, after all, it was a natural process. Other men's wives went through it unharmed, and why should not his? He was himself one of a family of fourteen, and yet his mother was alive and hearty. It was quite the exception for anything to go wrong. And yet in spite of his reasonings the remembrance of his wife's condition was always like a sombre background to all his other thoughts.

Doctor Miles of Bridport Place, the best man in the neighbourhood, was retained five months in advance, and, as time stole on, many little packets of absurdly small white garments with frill work and ribbons began to arrive among the big consignments of male necessities. And then one evening, as Johnson was ticketing the scarves in the shop, he heard a bustle upstairs, and Mrs. Peyton came running down to say that Lucy was bad and that she thought the doctor ought to be there without delay.

It was not Robert Johnson's nature to hurry. He was prim and staid and liked to do things in an orderly fashion. It was a quarter of a mile from the corner of the New North Road where his shop stood to the doctor's house in Bridport Place. There were no cabs in sight, so he set off upon foot, leaving the lad to mind the shop. At Bridport Place he was told that the doctor had just gone to Harman Street to attend a man in a fit. Johnson started off for Harman Street, losing a little of his primness as he became more anxious. Two full cabs but no empty ones passed him on the way. At Harman Street he learned that the doctor had gone on to a case of measles, fortunately he had left the address—69 Dunstan Road, at the other side of the Regent's Canal. Johnson's primness had vanished now as he thought of the women waiting at home, and he began to run as hard as he could down the Kingsland Road. Some way along he sprang into a cab which stood by the curb and drove to Dunstan Road. The doctor had just left, and Robert Johnson felt inclined to sit down upon the steps in despair.

Fortunately he had not sent the cab away, and he was soon back at Bridport Place. Doctor Miles had not returned yet, but they were expecting him every instant. Johnson waited, drumming his fingers on his knees, in a high, dim-lit room, the air of which was charged with a faint, sickly smell of ether. The furniture was massive, and the books in the shelves were sombre, and a squat black clock ticked mournfully on the mantelpiece. It told him that it was half-past seven, and that he had been gone an hour and a quarter. Whatever would the women think of him! Every time that a distant door slammed he sprang from his chair in a quiver of eagerness. His ears strained to catch the deep notes of the doctor's voice. And then, suddenly, with a gush of joy he heard a quick step outside, and the sharp click of the key in the lock. In an instant he was out in the hall, before the doctor's foot was over the threshold.

"If you please, doctor, I've come for you," he cried; "the wife was taken bad at six o'clock."

He hardly knew what he expected the doctor to do. Something very energetic, certainly—to seize some drugs, perhaps, and rush excitedly with him through the gaslit streets. Instead of that Doctor Miles threw his umbrella into the rack, jerked off his hat with a somewhat peevish gesture, and pushed Johnson back into the room.

"Let's see! You did engage me, didn't you?" he asked in no very cordial voice.

"Oh yes, doctor, last November. Johnson, the outfitter, you know, in the New North Road."

"Yes, yes. It's a bit overdue," said the doctor, glancing at a list of names in a note-book with a very shiny cover. "Well, how is she?"

"I don't——"

"Ah, of course, it's your first. You'll know more about it next time."

"Mrs. Peyton said it was time you were there, sir."

"My dear sir, there can be no very pressing hurry in a first case. We shall have an all-night affair, I fancy. You can't get an engine to go without coals, Mr. Johnson, and I have had nothing but a light lunch."

"We could have something cooked for you—something hot and a cup of tea."

"Thank you, but I fancy my dinner is actually on the table. I can do no good in the earlier stages. Go home and say that I am coming, and I will be round immediately afterwards."

A sort of horror filled Robert Johnson as he gazed at this man who could think about his dinner at such a moment. He had not imagination enough to realise that the experience which seemed so appallingly important to him, was the merest everyday matter of business to the medical man who could not have lived for a year had he not, amid the rush of work, remembered what was due to his own health. To Johnson he seemed little better than a monster. His thoughts were bitter as he sped back to his shop.

"You've taken your time," said his mother-in-law reproachfully, looking down the stairs as he entered.

"I couldn't help it!" he gasped. "Is it over?"

"Over! She's got to be worse, poor dear, before she can be better. Where's Doctor Miles?"

"He's coming after he's had dinner."

The old woman was about to make some reply, when, from the half-opened door behind, a high, whinnying voice cried out for her. She ran back and closed the door, while Johnson, sick at heart, turned into the shop. There he sent the lad home and busied himself frantically in putting up shutters and turning out boxes. When all was closed and finished he seated himself in the parlour behind the shop. But he could not sit still. He rose incessantly to walk a few paces and then fall back into a chair once more. Suddenly the clatter of china fell upon his ear, and he saw the maid pass the door with a cup on a tray and a smoking teapot.

"Who is that for, Jane?" he asked.

"For the mistress, Mr. Johnson. She says she would fancy it."

There was immeasurable consolation to him in that homely cup of tea. It wasn't so very bad after all if his wife could think of such things. So lighthearted was he that he asked for a cup also. He had just finished it when the doctor arrived, with a small black-leather bag in his hand.

"Well, how is she?" he asked genially.

"Oh, she's very much better," said Johnson, with enthusiasm.

"Dear me, that's bad!" said the doctor. "Perhaps it will do if I look in on my morning round?"

"No, no," cried Johnson, clutching at his thick frieze overcoat. "We are so glad that you have come. And, doctor, please come down soon and let me know what you think about it."

The doctor passed upstairs, his firm, heavy steps resounding through the house. Johnson could hear his boots creaking as he walked about the floor above him, and the sound was a consolation to him. It was crisp and decided, the tread of a man who had plenty of self-confidence. Presently, still straining his ears to catch what was going on, he heard the scraping of a chair as it was drawn along the floor, and a moment later he heard the door fly open, and some one came rushing downstairs. Johnson sprang up with his hair bristling, thinking that some dreadful thing had occurred, but it was only his mother-in-law, incoherent with excitement and searching for scissors and some tape. She vanished again and Jane passed up the stairs with a pile of newly-aired linen. Then, after an interval of silence, Johnson heard the heavy, creaking tread and the doctor came down into the parlour.

"That's better," said he, pausing with his hand upon the door. "You look pale, Mr. Johnson."

"Oh no, sir, not at all," he answered deprecatingly, mopping his brow with his handkerchief.

"There is no immediate cause for alarm," said Doctor Miles. "The case is not all that we could wish it. Still we will hope for the best."

"Is there danger, sir?" gasped Johnson.

"Well, there is always danger, of course. It is not altogether a favourable case, but still it might be much worse. I have given her a draught. I saw as I passed that they have been doing a little building opposite to you. It's an improving quarter. The rents go higher and higher. You have a lease of your own little place, eh?"

"Yes, sir, yes!" cried Johnson, whose ears were straining for every sound from above, and who felt none the less that it was very soothing that the doctor should be able to chat so easily at such a time. "That's to say no, sir, I am a yearly tenant."

"Ah, I should get a lease if I were you. There's Marshall, the watchmaker, down the street, I attended his wife twice and saw him through the typhoid when they took up the drains in Prince Street. I assure you his landlord sprung his rent nearly forty a year and he had to pay or clear out."

"Did his wife get through it, doctor?"

"Oh yes, she did very well. Hullo! Hullo!"

He slanted his ear to the ceiling with a questioning face, and then darted swiftly from the room.

It was March and the evenings were chill, so Jane had lit the fire, but the wind drove the smoke downwards and the air was full of its acrid taint. Johnson felt chilled to the bone, though rather by his apprehensions than by the weather. He crouched over the fire with his thin white hands held out to the blaze. At ten o'clock Jane brought in the joint of cold meat and laid his place for supper, but he could not bring himself to touch it. He drank a glass of the beer, however, and felt the better for it. The tension of his nerves seemed to have reacted upon his hearing, and he was able to follow the most trivial things in the room above. Once, when the beer was still heartening him, he nerved himself to creep on tiptoe up the stair and to listen to what was going on. The bedroom door was half an inch open, and through the slit he could catch a glimpse of the clean-shaven face of the doctor, looking wearier and more anxious than before. Then he rushed downstairs like a lunatic, and running to the door he tried to distract his thoughts by watching what was going on in the street. The shops were all shut, and some rollicking boon companions came shouting along from the public-house. He stayed at the door until the stragglers had thinned down, and then came back to his seat by the fire. In his dim brain he was asking himself questions which had never intruded themselves before. Where was the justice of it? What had his sweet, innocent little wife done that she should be used so? Why was Nature so cruel? He was frightened at his own thoughts, and yet wondered that they had never occurred to him before.

As the early morning drew in, Johnson, sick at heart and shivering in every limb, sat with his great-coat huddled round him, staring at the grey ashes and waiting hopelessly for some relief. His face was white and clammy, and his nerves had been numbed into a half-conscious state by the long monotony of misery. But suddenly all his feelings leapt into keen life again as he heard the bedroom door open and the doctor's steps upon the stair. Robert Johnson was precise and unemotional in everyday life, but he almost shrieked now as he rushed forward to know if it were over.

One glance at the stern, drawn face which met him showed that it was no pleasant news which had sent the doctor downstairs. His appearance had altered as much as Johnson's during the last few hours. His hair was on end, his face flushed, his forehead dotted with beads of perspiration. There was a peculiar fierceness in his eye, and about the lines of his mouth, a fighting look as befitted a man who for hours on end had been striving with the hungriest of foes for the most precious of prizes. But there was a sadness too, as though his grim opponent had been overmastering him. He sat down and leaned his head upon his hand like a man who is fagged out.

"I thought it my duty to see you, Mr. Johnson, and to tell you that it is a very nasty case. Your wife's heart is not strong, and she has some symptoms which I do not like. What I wanted to say is that if you would like to have a second opinion I shall be very glad to meet any one whom you might suggest."

Johnson was so dazed by his want of sleep and the evil news that he could hardly grasp the doctor's meaning. The other, seeing him hesitate, thought that he was considering the expense.

"Smith or Hawley would come for two guineas," said he. "But I think Pritchard of the City Road is the best man."

"Oh yes, bring the best man," cried Johnson.

"Pritchard would want three guineas. He is a senior man, you see."

"I'd give him all I have if he would pull her through. Shall I run for him?"

"Yes. Go to my house first and ask for the green baize bag. The assistant will give it to you. Tell him I want the A.C.E. mixture. Her heart is too weak for chloroform. Then go for Pritchard and bring him back with you."

It was heavenly for Johnson to have something to do and to feel that he was of some use to his wife. He ran swiftly to Bridport Place, his footfalls clattering through the silent streets, and the big dark policemen turning their yellow funnels of light on him as he passed. Two tugs at the night-bell brought down a sleepy, half-clad assistant, who handed him a stoppered glass bottle and a cloth bag which contained something which clinked when you moved it. Johnson thrust the bottle into his pocket, seized the green bag, and pressing his hat firmly down ran as hard as he could set foot to ground until he was in the City Road and saw the name of Pritchard engraved in white upon a red ground. He bounded in triumph up the three steps which led to the door, and as he did so there was a crash behind him. His precious bottle was in fragments upon the pavement.

For a moment he felt as if it were his wife's body that was lying there. But the run had freshened his wits and he saw that the mischief might be repaired. He pulled vigorously at the night-bell.

"Well, what's the matter?" asked a gruff voice at his elbow. He started back and looked up at the windows, but there was no sign of life. He was approaching the bell again with the intention of pulling it, when a perfect roar burst from the wall.

"I can't stand shivering here all night," cried the voice. "Say who you are and what you want or I shut the tube."

Then for the first time Johnson saw that the end of a speaking tube hung out of the wall just above the bell. He shouted up it—

"I want you to come with me to meet Doctor Miles at a confinement at once."

"How far?" shrieked the irascible voice.

"The New North Road, Hoxton."

"My consultation fee is three guineas, payable at the time."

"All right," shouted Johnson. "You are to bring a bottle of A.C.E. mixture with you."

"All right! Wait a bit!"

Five minutes later an elderly, hard-faced man with grizzled hair flung open the door. As he emerged a voice from somewhere in the shadows cried—

"Mind you take your cravat, John," and he impatiently growled something over his shoulder in reply.

The consultant was a man who had been hardened by a life of ceaseless labour, and who had been driven, as so many others have been, by the needs of his own increasing family to set the commercial before the philanthropic side of his profession. Yet beneath his rough crust he was a man with a kindly heart.

"We don't want to break a record," said he, pulling up and panting after attempting to keep up with Johnson for five minutes. "I would go quicker if I could, my dear sir, and I quite sympathise with your anxiety, but really I can't manage it."

So Johnson, on fire with impatience, had to slow down until they reached the New North Road, when he ran ahead and had the door open for the doctor when he came. He heard the two meet outside the bedroom, and caught scraps of their conversation. "Sorry to knock you up—nasty case—decent people." Then it sank into a mumble and the door closed behind them.

Johnson sat up in his chair now, listening keenly, for he knew that a crisis must be at hand. He heard the two doctors moving about, and was able to distinguish the step of Pritchard, which had a drag in it, from the clean, crisp sound of the other's footfall. There was silence for a few minutes and then a curious drunken, mumbling sing-song voice came quavering up, very unlike anything which he had heard hitherto. At the same time a sweetish, insidious scent, imperceptible perhaps to any nerves less strained than his, crept down the stairs and penetrated into the room. The voice dwindled into a mere drone and finally sank away into silence, and Johnson gave a long sigh of relief for he knew that the drug had done its work and that, come what might, there should be no more pain for the sufferer.

But soon the silence became even more trying to him than the cries had been. He had no clue now as to what was going on, and his mind swarmed with horrible possibilities. He rose and went to the bottom of the stairs again. He heard the clink of metal against metal, and the subdued murmur of the doctors' voices. Then he heard Mrs. Peyton say something, in a tone as of fear or expostulation, and again the doctors murmured together. For twenty minutes he stood there leaning against the wall, listening to the occasional rumbles of talk without being able to catch a word of it. And then of a sudden there rose out of the silence the strangest little piping cry, and Mrs. Peyton screamed out in her delight and the man ran into the parlour and flung himself down upon the horse-hair sofa, drumming his heels on it in his ecstasy.

But often the great cat Fate lets us go, only to clutch us again in a fiercer grip. As minute after minute passed and still no sound came from above save those thin, glutinous cries, Johnson cooled from his frenzy of joy, and lay breathless with his ears straining. They were moving slowly about. They were talking in subdued tones. Still minute after minute passing, and no word from the voice for which he listened. His nerves were dulled by his night of trouble, and he waited in limp wretchedness upon his sofa. There he still sat when the doctors came down to him—a bedraggled, miserable figure with his face grimy and his hair unkempt from his long vigil. He rose as they entered, bracing himself against the mantelpiece.

"Is she dead?" he asked.

"Doing well," answered the doctor.

And at the words that little conventional spirit which had never known until that night the capacity for fierce agony which lay within it, learned for the second time that there were springs of joy also which it had never tapped before. His impulse was to fall upon his knees, but he was shy before the doctors.

"Can I go up?"

"In a few minutes."

"I'm sure, doctor. I'm very—I'm very——" he grew inarticulate. "Here are your three guineas, Doctor Pritchard. I wish they were three hundred."

"So do I," said the senior man, and they laughed as they shook hands.

Johnson opened the shop door for them and heard their talk as they stood for an instant outside.

"Looked nasty at one time."

"Very glad to have your help."

"Delighted, I'm sure. Won't you step round and have a cup of coffee?"

"No, thanks. I'm expecting another case."

The firm step and the dragging one passed away to the right and the left. Johnson turned from the door still with that turmoil of joy in his heart. He seemed to be making a new start in life. He felt that he was a stronger and a deeper man. Perhaps all this suffering had an object then. It might prove to be a blessing both to his wife and to him. The very thought was one which he would have been incapable of conceiving twelve hours before. He was full of new emotions. If there had been a harrowing, there had been a planting too.

"Can I come up?" he cried, and then, without waiting for an answer, he took the steps three at a time.

Mrs. Peyton was standing by a soapy bath with a bundle in her hands. From under the curve of a brown shawl there looked out at him the strangest little red face with crumpled features, moist, loose lips, and eyelids which quivered like a rabbit's nostrils. The weak neck had let the head topple over, and it rested upon the shoulder.

"Kiss it, Robert!" cried the grandmother. "Kiss your son!"

But he felt a resentment to the little, red, blinking creature. He could not forgive it yet for that long night of misery. He caught sight of a white face in the bed and he ran towards it with such love and pity as his speech could find no words for.

"Thank God it is over! Lucy, dear, it was dreadful!"

"But I'm so happy now. I never was so happy in my life."

Her eyes were fixed upon the brown bundle.

"You mustn't talk," said Mrs. Peyton.

"But don't leave me," whispered his wife.

So he sat in silence with his hand in hers. The lamp was burning dim and the first cold light of dawn was breaking through the window. The night had been long and dark but the day was the sweeter and the purer in consequence. London was waking up. The roar began to rise from the street. Lives had come and lives had gone, but the great machine was still working out its dim and tragic destiny.

XII

A MEDICAL DOCUMENT

Medical men are, as a class, very much too busy to take stock of singular situations or dramatic events. Thus it happens that the ablest chronicler of their experiences in our literature was a lawyer. A life spent in watching over death-beds—or over birth-beds which are infinitely more trying—takes something from a man's sense of proportion, as constant strong waters might corrupt his palate. The overstimulated nerve ceases to respond. Ask the surgeon for his best experiences and he may reply that he has seen little that is remarkable, or break away into the technical. But catch him some night when the fire has spurted up and his pipe is reeking, with a few of his brother practitioners for company and an artful question or allusion to set him going. Then you will get some raw, green facts new plucked from the tree of life.

It is after one of the quarterly dinners of the Midland Branch of the British Medical Association. Twenty coffee cups, a dozen liqueur glasses, and a solid bank of blue smoke which swirls slowly along the high, gilded ceiling gives a hint of a successful gathering. But the members have shredded off to their homes. The line of heavy, bulge-pocketed overcoats and of stethoscope-bearing top hats is gone from the hotel corridor. Round the fire in the sitting-room three medicos are still lingering, however, all smoking and arguing, while a fourth, who is a mere layman and young at that, sits back at the table. Under cover of an open journal he is writing furiously with a stylographic pen, asking a question in an innocent voice from time to time and so flickering up the conversation whenever it shows a tendency to wane.

The three men are all of that staid middle age which begins early and lasts late in the profession. They are none of them famous, yet each is of good repute, and a fair type of his particular branch. The portly man with the authoritative manner and the white, vitriol splash upon his cheek is Charley Manson, chief of the Wormley Asylum, and author of the brilliant monograph—"Obscure Nervous Lesions in the Unmarried." He always wears his collar high like that, since the half-successful attempt of a student of Revelations to cut his throat with a splinter of glass. The second, with the ruddy face and the merry brown eyes, is a general practitioner, a man of vast experience, who, with his three assistants and his five horses, takes twenty-five hundred a year in half-crown visits and shilling consultations out of the poorest quarter of a great city. That cheery face of Theodore Foster is seen at the side of a hundred sick-beds a day, and if he has one-third more names on his visiting list than in his cash-book he always promises himself that he will get level some day when a millionaire with a chronic complaint—the ideal combination—shall seek his services. The third, sitting on the right with his dress-shoes shining on the top of the fender, is Hargrave, the rising surgeon. His face has none of the broad humanity of Theodore Foster's, the eye is stern and critical, the mouth straight and severe, but there is strength and decision in every line of it, and it is nerve rather than sympathy which the patient demands when he is bad enough to come to Hargrave's door. He calls himself a jawman, "a mere jawman," as he modestly puts it, but in point of fact he is too young and too poor to confine himself to a specialty, and there is nothing surgical which Hargrave has not the skill and the audacity to do.

"Before, after, and during," murmurs the general practitioner in answer to some interpolation of the outsider's. "I assure you, Manson, one sees all sorts of evanescent forms of madness."

"Ah, puerperal!" throws in the other, knocking the curved grey ash from his cigar. "But you had some case in your mind, Foster."

"Well, there was one only last week which was new to me. I had been engaged by some people of the name of Silcoe. When the trouble came round I went myself, for they would not hear of an assistant. The husband, who was a policeman, was sitting at the head of the bed on the further side. 'This won't do,' said I. 'Oh yes, doctor, it must do,' said she. 'It's quite irregular, and he must go,' said I. 'It's that or nothing,' said she. 'I won't open my mouth or stir a finger the whole night,' said he. So it ended by my allowing him to remain, and there he sat for eight hours on end. She was very good over the matter, but every now and again he would fetch a hollow groan, and I noticed that he held his right hand just under the sheet all the time, where I had no doubt that it was clasped by her left. When it was all happily over, I looked at him and his face was the colour of this cigar ash, and his head had dropped on to the edge of the pillow. Of course I thought he had fainted with emotion, and I was just telling myself what I thought of myself for having been such a fool as to let him stay there, when suddenly I saw that the sheet over his hand was all soaked with blood; I whisked it down, and there was the fellow's wrist half cut through. The woman had one bracelet of a policeman's handcuff over her left wrist and the other round his right one. When she had been in pain she had twisted with all her strength and the iron had fairly eaten into the bone of the man's arm. 'Aye, doctor,' said she, when she saw I had noticed it. 'He's got to take his share as well as me. Turn and turn,' said she."

"Don't you find it a very wearing branch of the profession?" asks Foster after a pause.

"My dear fellow, it was the fear of it that drove me into lunacy work."

"Aye, and it has driven men into asylums who never found their way on to the medical staff. I was a very shy fellow myself as a student, and I know what it means."

"No joke that in general practice," says the alienist.

"Well, you hear men talk about it as though it were, but I tell you it's much nearer tragedy. Take some poor, raw, young fellow who has just put up his plate in a strange town. He has found it a trial all his life, perhaps, to talk to a woman about lawn tennis and church services. When a young man is shy he is shyer than any girl. Then down comes an anxious mother and consults him upon the most intimate family matters. 'I shall never go to that doctor again,' says she afterwards. 'His manner is so stiff and unsympathetic.' Unsympathetic! Why, the poor lad was struck dumb and paralysed. I have known general practitioners who were so shy that they could not bring themselves to ask the way in the street. Fancy what sensitive men like that must endure before they get broken in to medical practice. And then they know that nothing is so catching as shyness, and that if they do not keep a face of stone, their patient will be covered with confusion. And so they keep their face of stone, and earn the reputation perhaps of having a heart to correspond. I suppose nothing would shake your nerve, Manson."

"Well, when a man lives year in year out among a thousand lunatics, with a fair sprinkling of homicidals among them, one's nerves either get set or shattered. Mine are all right so far."

"I was frightened once," says the surgeon. "It was when I was doing dispensary work. One night I had a call from some very poor people, and gathered from the few words they said that their child was ill. When I entered the room I saw a small cradle in the corner. Raising the lamp I walked over and putting back the curtains I looked down at the baby. I tell you it was sheer Providence that I didn't drop that lamp and set the whole place alight. The head on the pillow turned, and I saw a face looking up at me which seemed to me to have more malignancy and wickedness than ever I had dreamed of in a nightmare. It was the flush of red over the cheek-bones, and the brooding eyes full of loathing of me, and of everything else, that impressed me. I'll never forget my start as, instead of the chubby face of an infant, my eyes fell upon this creature. I took the mother into the next room. 'What is it?' I asked. 'A girl of sixteen,' said she, and then throwing up her arms, 'Oh, pray God she may be taken!' The poor thing, though she spent her life in this little cradle, had great, long, thin limbs which she curled up under her. I lost sight of the case and don't know what became of it, but I'll never forget the look in her eyes."

"That's creepy," says Doctor Foster. "But I think one of my experiences would run it close. Shortly after I put up my plate I had a visit from a little hunch-backed woman, who wished me to come and attend to her sister in her trouble. When I reached the house, which was a very poor one, I found two other little hunched-backed women, exactly like the first, waiting for me in the sitting-room. Not one of them said a word, but my companion took the lamp and walked upstairs with her two sisters behind her, and me bringing up the rear. I can see those three queer shadows cast by the lamp upon the wall as clearly as I can see that tobacco pouch. In the room above was the fourth sister, a remarkably beautiful girl in evident need of my assistance. There was no wedding ring upon her finger. The three deformed sisters seated themselves round the room, like so many graven images, and all night not one of them opened her mouth. I'm not romancing, Hargrave; this is absolute fact. In the early morning a fearful thunderstorm broke out, one of the most violent I have ever known. The little garret burned blue with the lightning, and the thunder roared and rattled as if it were on the very roof of the house. It wasn't much of a lamp I had, and it was a queer thing when a spurt of lightning came to see those three twisted figures sitting round the walls, or to have the voice of my patient drowned by the booming of the thunder. By Jove, I don't mind telling you that there was a time when I nearly bolted from the room. All came right in the end, but I never heard the true story of the unfortunate beauty and her three crippled sisters."

"That's the worst of these medical stories," sighs the outsider. "They never seem to have an end."

"When a man is up to his neck in practice, my boy, he has no time to gratify his private curiosity. Things shoot across him and he gets a glimpse of them, only to recall them, perhaps, at some quiet moment like this. But I've always felt, Manson, that your line had as much of the terrible in it as any other."

"More," groans the alienist. "A disease of the body is bad enough, but this seems to be a disease of the soul. Is it not a shocking thing—a thing to drive a reasoning man into absolute Materialism—to think that you may have a fine, noble fellow with every divine instinct and that some little vascular change, the dropping, we will say, of a minute spicule of bone from the inner table of his skull on to the surface of his brain may have the effect of changing him to a filthy and pitiable creature with every low and debasing tendency? What a satire an asylum is upon the majesty of man, and no less upon the ethereal nature of the soul."

"Faith and hope," murmurs the general practitioner.

"I have no faith, not much hope, and all the charity I can afford," says the surgeon. "When theology squares itself with the facts of life I'll read it up."

"You were talking about cases," says the outsider, jerking the ink down into his stylographic pen.

"Well, take a common complaint which kills many thousands every year, like G.P. for instance."

"What's G.P.?"

"General practitioner," suggests the surgeon with a grin.

"The British public will have to know what G.P. is," says the alienist gravely. "It's increasing by leaps and bounds, and it has the distinction of being absolutely incurable. General paralysis is its full title, and I tell you it promises to be a perfect scourge. Here's a fairly typical case now which I saw last Monday week. A young farmer, a splendid fellow, surprised his friends by taking a very rosy view of things at a time when the whole country-side was grumbling. He was going to give up wheat, give up arable land, too, if it didn't pay, plant two thousand acres of rhododendrons and get a monopoly of the supply for Covent Garden—there was no end to his schemes, all sane enough but just a bit inflated. I called at the farm, not to see him, but on an altogether different matter. Something about the man's way of talking struck me and I watched him narrowly. His lip had a trick of quivering, his words slurred themselves together, and so did his handwriting when he had occasion to draw up a small agreement. A closer inspection showed me that one of his pupils was ever so little larger than the other. As I left the house his wife came after me. 'Isn't it splendid to see Job looking so well, doctor?' said she; 'he's that full of energy he can hardly keep himself quiet.' I did not say anything, for I had not the heart, but I knew that the fellow was as much condemned to death as though he were lying in the cell at Newgate. It was a characteristic case of incipient G.P."

"Good heavens!" cries the outsider. "My own lips tremble. I often slur my words. I believe I've got it myself."

Three little chuckles come from the front of the fire.

"There's the danger of a little medical knowledge to the layman."

"A great authority has said that every first year's student is suffering in silent agony from four diseases," remarks the surgeon. "One is heart disease, of course; another is cancer of the parotid. I forget the two other."

"Where does the parotid come in?"

"Oh, it's the last wisdom tooth coming through!"

"And what would be the end of that young farmer?" asks the outsider.

"Paresis of all the muscles, ending in fits, coma and death. It may be a few months, it may be a year or two. He was a very strong young man and would take some killing."

"By the way," says the alienist, "did I ever tell you about the first certificate I ever signed? I stood as near ruin then as a man could go."

"What was it, then?"

"I was in practice at the time. One morning a Mrs. Cooper called upon me and informed me that her husband had shown signs of delusions lately. They took the form of imagining that he had been in the army and had distinguished himself very much. As a matter of fact he was a lawyer and had never been out of England. Mrs. Cooper was of opinion that if I were to call it might alarm him, so it was agreed between us that she should send him up in the evening on some pretext to my consulting-room, which would give me the opportunity of having a chat with him and, if I were convinced of his insanity, of signing his certificate. Another doctor had already signed, so that it only needed my concurrence to have him placed under treatment. Well, Mr. Cooper arrived in the evening about half an hour before I had expected him, and consulted me as to some malarious symptoms from which he said that he suffered.

According to his account he had just returned from the Abyssinian Campaign, and had been one of the first of the British forces to enter Magdala. No delusion could possibly be more marked, for he would talk of little else, so I filled in the papers without the slightest hesitation. When his wife arrived, after he had left, I put some questions to her to complete the forms. 'What is his age?' I asked. 'Fifty,' said she. 'Fifty!' I cried. 'Why, the man I examined could not have been more than thirty!' And so it came out that the real Mr. Cooper had never called upon me at all, but that by one of those coincidences which takes a man's breath away another Cooper, who really was a very distinguished young officer of artillery, had come in to consult me. My pen was wet to sign the paper when I discovered it," says Dr. Manson, mopping his forehead.

"We were talking about nerve just now," observes the surgeon. "Just, after my qualifying I served in the Navy for a time, as I think you know. I was on the flag-ship on the West African Station, and I remember a singular example of nerve which came to my notice at that time. One of our small gunboats had gone up the Calabar river, and when there the surgeon died of coast fever. On the same day a man's leg was broken by a spar falling upon it, and it became quite obvious that it must be taken off above the knee if his life was to be saved. The young lieutenant who was in charge of the craft searched among the dead doctor's effects and laid his hands upon some chloroform, a hip-joint knife, and a volume of Grey's Anatomy. He had the man laid by the steward upon the cabin table, and with a picture of the cross section of the thigh in front of him he began to take off the limb. Every now and then, referring to the diagram, he would say: 'Stand by with the lashings, steward. There's blood on the chart about here.' Then he would jab with his knife until he cut the artery, and he and his assistant would tie it up before they went any further. In this way they gradually whittled the leg off, and upon my word they made a very excellent job of it. The man is hopping about the Portsmouth Yard at this day.

"It's no joke when the doctor of one of these isolated gunboats himself falls ill," continues the surgeon after a pause. "You might think it easy for him to prescribe for himself, but this fever knocks you down like a club, and you haven't strength left to brush a mosquito off your face. I had a touch of it at Lagos, and I know what I am telling you. But there was a chum of mine who really had a curious experience. The whole crew gave him up, and, as they had never had a funeral aboard the ship, they began rehearsing the forms so as to be ready. They thought that he was unconscious, but he swears he could hear every word that passed. 'Corpse comin' up the 'atchway!' cried the cockney sergeant of Marines. 'Present harms!' He was so amused, and so indignant too, that he just made up his mind that he wouldn't be carried through that hatchway, and he wasn't, either."

"There's no need for fiction in medicine," remarks Foster, "for the facts will always beat anything you can fancy. But it has seemed to me sometimes that a curious paper might be read at some of these meetings about the uses of medicine in popular fiction."

"How?"

"Well, of what the folk die of, and what diseases are made most use of in novels. Some are worn to pieces, and others, which are equally common in real life, are never mentioned. Typhoid is fairly frequent, but scarlet fever is unknown. Heart disease is common, but then heart disease, as we know it, is usually the sequel of some foregoing disease, of which we never hear anything in the romance. Then there is the mysterious malady called brain fever, which always attacks the heroine after a crisis, but which is unknown under that name to the text books. People when they are over-excited in novels fall down in a fit. In a fairly large experience I have never known any one to do so in real life. The small complaints simply don't exist. Nobody ever gets shingles or quinsy, or mumps in a novel. All the diseases, too, belongs to the upper part of the body. The novelist never strikes below the belt."

"I'll tell you what, Foster," says the alienist, "there is a side of life which is too medical for the general public and too romantic for the professional journals, but which contains some of the richest human materials that a man could study. It's not a pleasant side, I am afraid, but if it is good enough for Providence to create, it is good enough for us to try and understand. It would deal with strange outbursts of savagery and vice in the lives of the best men, curious momentary weaknesses in the record of the sweetest women, known but to one or two, and inconceivable to the world around. It would deal, too, with the singular phenomena of waxing and of waning manhood, and would throw a light upon those actions which have cut short many an honoured career and sent a man to a prison when he should have been hurried to a consulting-room. Of all evils that may come upon the sons of men, God shield us principally from that one!"

"I had a case some little time ago which was out of the ordinary," says the surgeon. "There was a famous beauty in London Society—I mention no names—who used to be remarkable a few seasons ago for the very low dresses which she would wear. She had the whitest of skins, and most beautiful of shoulders, so it was no wonder. Then gradually the frilling at her neck lapped upwards and upwards, until last year she astonished every one by wearing quite a high collar at a time when it was completely out of fashion. Well, one day this very woman was shown into my consulting-room. When the footman was gone she suddenly tore off the upper part of her dress. 'For God's sake do something for me!' she cried. Then I saw what the trouble was. A rodent ulcer was eating its way upwards, coiling on in its serpiginous fashion until the end of it was flush with her collar. The red streak of its trail was lost below the line of her bust. Year by year it had ascended and she had heightened her dress to hide it, until now it was about to invade her face. She had been too proud to confess her trouble, even to a medical man."

"And did you stop it?"

"Well, with zinc chloride I did what I could. But it may break out again. She was one of those beautiful white-and-pink creatures who are rotten with struma. You may patch but you can't mend."

"Dear! dear! dear!" cries the general practitioner, with that kindly softening of the eyes which has endeared him to so many thousands. "I suppose we mustn't think ourselves wiser than

Providence, but there are times when one feels that something is wrong in the scheme of things. I've seen some sad things in my life. Did I ever tell you that case where Nature divorced a most loving couple? He was a fine young fellow, an athlete and a gentleman, but he overdid athletics. You know how the force that controls us gives us a little tweak to remind us when we get off the beaten track. It may be a pinch on the great toe if we drink too much and work too little. Or it may be a tug on our nerves if we dissipate energy too much. With the athlete, of course, it's the heart or the lungs. He had bad phthisis and was sent to Davos. Well, as luck would have it, she developed rheumatic fever, which left her heart very much affected. Now, do you see the dreadful dilemma in which those poor people found themselves? When he came below 4,000 feet or so, his symptoms became terrible. She could come up about 2,500, and then her heart reached its limit. They had several interviews half-way down the valley, which left them nearly dead, and at last, the doctors had to absolutely forbid it. And so for four years they lived within three miles of each other and never met. Every morning he would go to a place which overlooked the chalet in which she lived and would wave a great white cloth and she answer from below. They could see each other quite plainly with their field glasses, and they might have been in different planets for all their chance of meeting."

"And one at last died," says the outsider.

"No, sir. I'm sorry not to be able to clinch the story, but the man recovered and is now a successful stockbroker in Drapers Gardens. The woman, too, is the mother of a considerable family. But what are you doing there?"

"Only taking a note or two of your talk."

The three medical men laugh as they walk towards their overcoats.

"Why, we've done nothing but talk shop," says the general practitioner. "What possible interest can the public take in that?"

XIII

THE SURGEON TALKS

"Men die of the diseases which they have studied most," remarked the surgeon, snipping off the end of a cigar with all his professional neatness and finish. "It's as if the morbid condition was an evil creature which, when it found itself closely hunted, flew at the throat of its pursuer. If you worry the microbes too much they may worry you. I've seen cases of it, and not necessarily in microbic diseases either. There was, of course, the well-known instance of Liston and the aneurism; and a dozen others that I could mention. You couldn't have a clearer case than that of poor old Walker of St. Christopher's. Not heard of it? Well, of course, it was a little before your time, but I wonder that it should have been forgotten. You youngsters are so busy in keeping up to the day that you lose a good deal that is interesting of yesterday.

"Walker was one of the best men in Europe on nervous disease. You must have read his little book on sclerosis of the posterior columns. It's as interesting as a novel, and epoch-making in its way. He worked like a horse, did Walker—huge consulting practice—hours a day in the clinical wards—constant original investigations. And then he enjoyed himself also. 'De mortuis,' of course, but still it's an open secret among all who knew him. If he died at forty-five, he crammed eighty years into it. The marvel was that he could have held on so long at the pace at which he was going. But he took it beautifully when it came.

"I was his clinical assistant at the time. Walker was lecturing on locomotor ataxia to a wardful of youngsters. He was explaining that one of the early signs of the complaint was that the patient could not put his heels together with his eyes shut without staggering. As he spoke, he suited the action to the word. I don't suppose the boys noticed anything. I did, and so did he, though he finished his lecture without a sign.

"When it was over he came into my room and lit a cigaretto.

"'Just run over my reflexes, Smith,' said he.

"There was hardly a trace of them left, I tapped away at his knee-tendon and might as well have tried to get a jerk out of that sofa-cushion. He stood, with his eyes shut again, and he swayed like a bush in the wind.

"'So,' said he, 'it was not intercostal neuralgia after all.'

"Then I knew that he had had the lightning pains, and that the case was complete. There was nothing to say, so I sat looking at him while he puffed and puffed at the cigarette. Here he was, a man in the prime of life, one of the handsomest men in London, with money, fame, social success, everything at his feet, and now, without a moment's warning, he was told that inevitable death lay before him, a death accompanied by more refined and lingering tortures than if he were bound upon a Red Indian stake. He sat in the middle of the blue cigarette cloud with his eyes cast down, and the slightest little tightening of his lips. Then he rose with a motion of his arms, as one who throws off old thoughts and enters upon a new course.

"'Better put this thing straight at once,' said he. 'I must make some fresh arrangements. May I use your paper and envelopes?'

"He settled himself at my desk and he wrote half a dozen letters. It is not a breach of confidence to say that they were not addressed to his professional brothers. Walker was a single man, which means that he was not restricted to a single woman. When he had finished, he walked out of that little room of mine, leaving every hope and ambition of his life behind him. And he might have had another year of ignorance and peace if it had not been for the chance illustration in his lecture.

"It took five years to kill him, and he stood it well. If he had ever been a little irregular he atoned for it in that long martyrdom. He kept an admirable record of his own symptoms, and worked out the eye changes more fully than has ever been done. When the ptosis got very bad he would hold his eyelid up with one hand while he wrote. Then, when he could not co-ordinate his muscles to write, he dictated to his nurse. So died, in the odour of science, James Walker, æt. 45.

"Poor old Walker was very fond of experimental surgery, and he broke ground in several directions. Between ourselves, there may have been some more ground-breaking afterwards, but he did his best for his cases. You know M'Namara, don't you? He always wears his hair long. He lets it be understood that it comes from his artistic strain, but it is really to conceal the loss of one of his ears. Walker cut the other one off, but you must not tell Mac I said so.

"It was like this. Walker had a fad about the portio dura—the motor to the face, you know—and he thought paralysis of it came from a disturbance of the blood supply. Something else which counterbalanced that disturbance might, he thought, set it right again. We had a very obstinate case of Bell's paralysis in the wards, and had tried it with every conceivable thing, blistering, tonics, nerve-stretching, galvanism, needles, but all without result. Walker got it into his head that removal of the ear would increase the blood supply to the part, and he very soon gained the consent of the patient to the operation.

"Well, we did it at night. Walker, of course, felt that it was something of an experiment, and did not wish too much talk about it unless it proved successful. There were half a dozen of us there, M'Namara and I among the rest. The room was a small one, and in the centre was the narrow table, with a mackintosh over the pillow, and a blanket which extended almost to the floor on either side. Two candles, on a side-table near the pillow, supplied all the light. In came the patient, with one side of his face as smooth as a baby's, and the other all in a quiver with fright. He lay down, and the chloroform towel was placed over his face, while Walker threaded his needles in the candle light. The chloroformist stood at the head of the table, and M'Namara was stationed at the side to control the patient. The rest of us stood by to assist.

"Well, the man was about half over when he fell into one of those convulsive flurries which come with the semi-unconscious stage. He kicked and plunged and struck out with both hands. Over with a crash went the little table which held the candles, and in an instant we were left in total darkness. You can think what a rush and a scurry there was, one to pick up the table, one to find the matches, and some to restrain the patient, who was still dashing himself about. He was held down by two dressers, the chloroform was pushed, and by the time the candles were relit, his incoherent, half-smothered shoutings had changed to a stertorous snore. His head was turned on the pillow and the towel was still kept over his face while the operation was carried through. Then the towel was withdrawn, and you can conceive our amazement when we looked upon the face of M'Namara.

"How did it happen? Why, simply enough. As the candles went over, the chloroformist had stopped for an instant and had tried to catch them. The patient, just as the light went out, had rolled off and under the table. Poor M'Namara, clinging frantically to him, had been dragged across it, and the chloroformist, feeling him there, had naturally clapped the towel across his mouth and nose. The others had secured him, and the more he roared and kicked the more they drenched him with chloroform. Walker was very nice about it, and made the most handsome apologies. He offered to do a plastic on the spot, and make as good an ear as he could, but M'Namara had had enough of it. As to the patient, we found him sleeping placidly under the table, with the ends of the blanket screening him on both sides. Walker sent M'Namara round his ear next day in a jar of methylated spirit, but Mac's wife was very angry about it, and it led to a good deal of ill-feeling. Some people say that the more one has to do with human nature, and the closer one is brought in contact with it, the less one thinks of it. I don't believe that those who know most would uphold that view. My own experience is dead against it. I was brought up in the miserable-mortal-clay school of theology, and yet here I am, after thirty years of intimate acquaintance with humanity, filled with respect for it. The evil lies commonly upon the surface. The deeper strata are good. A hundred times I have seen folk condemned to death as suddenly as poor Walker was. Sometimes it was to blindness or to mutilations which are worse than death. Men and women, they almost all took it beautifully, and some with such lovely unselfishness, and with such complete absorption in the thought of how their fate would affect others, that the man about town, or the frivolously-dressed woman had seemed to change into an angel before my eyes. I have seen death-beds, too, of all ages and of all creeds and want of creeds. I never saw any of them shrink, save only one poor, imaginative young fellow, who had spent his blameless life in the strictest of sects. Of course, an exhausted frame is incapable of fear, as any one can vouch who is told, in the midst of his seasickness, that the ship is going to the bottom. That is why I rate courage in the face of mutilation to be higher than courage when a wasting illness is fining away into death.

"Now, I'll take a case which I had in my own practice last Wednesday. A lady came in to consult me—the wife of a well-known sporting baronet. The husband had come with her, but remained, at her request, in the waiting-room. I need not go into details, but it proved to be a peculiarly malignant case of cancer. 'I knew it,' said she. 'How long have I to live?' 'I fear that it may exhaust your strength in a few months,' I answered. 'Poor old Jack!' said she. 'I'll tell him that it is not dangerous.' 'Why should you deceive him?' I asked. 'Well, he's very uneasy about it, and he is quaking now in the waiting-room. He has two old friends to dinner to-night, and I haven't the heart to spoil his evening. To-morrow will be time enough for him to learn the truth.' Out she walked, the brave little woman, and a moment later her husband, with his big, red face shining with joy came plunging into my room to shake me by the hand. No, I respected her wish and I did not undeceive him. I dare bet that evening was one of the brightest, and the next morning the darkest, of his life.

"It's wonderful how bravely and cheerily a woman can face a crushing blow. It is different with men. A man can stand it without, but it knocks him dazed and silly all the same. But the woman does not lose her wits any more than she does her courage. Now, I had a case only a few weeks ago which would show you what I mean. A gentleman consulted me about his wife, a very beautiful woman. She had a small tubercular nodule upon her upper arm, according to him. He was sure that it was of no importance, but he wanted to know whether Devonshire or the Riviera would be the better for her. I examined her and found a frightful sarcoma of the bone, hardly showing upon the surface, but involving the shoulder-blade and clavicle as well as the humerus. A more malignant case I have never seen. I sent her out of the room and I told him the truth.

What did he do? Why, he walked slowly round that room with his hands behind his back, looking with the greatest interest at the pictures. I can see him now, putting up his gold pince-nez and staring at them with perfectly vacant eyes, which told me that he saw neither them nor the wall behind them. 'Amputation of the arm?' he asked at last. 'And of the collar-bone and shoulder-blade,' said I. 'Quite so. The collar-bone and shoulder-blade,' he repeated, still staring about him with those lifeless eyes. It settled him. I don't believe he'll ever be the same man again. But the woman took it as bravely and brightly as could be, and she has done very well since. The mischief was so great that the arm snapped as we drew it from the night-dress. No, I don't think that there will be any return, and I have every hope of her recovery.

"The first patient is a thing which one remembers all one's life. Mine was commonplace, and the details are of no interest. I had a curious visitor, however, during the first few months after my plate went up. It was an elderly woman, richly dressed, with a wicker-work picnic basket in her hand. This she opened with the tears streaming down her face, and out there waddled the fattest, ugliest and mangiest little pug dog that I have ever seen. 'I wish you to put him painlessly out of the world, doctor,' she cried. 'Quick, quick, or my resolution may give way.' She flung herself down, with hysterical sobs, upon the sofa. The less experienced a doctor is, the higher are his notions of professional dignity, as I need not remind you, my young friend, so I was about to refuse the commission with indignation, when I bethought me that, quite apart from medicine, we were gentleman and lady, and that she had asked me to do something for her which was evidently of the greatest possible importance in her eyes. I led off the poor little doggie, therefore, and with the help of a saucerful of milk and a few drops of prussic acid his exit was as speedy and painless as could be desired. 'Is it over?' she cried as I entered. It was really tragic to see how all the love which should have gone to husband and children had, in default of them, been centred upon this uncouth little animal. She left, quite broken down, in her carriage, and it was only after her departure that I saw an envelope sealed with a large red seal, and lying upon the blotting pad of my desk. Outside, in pencil, was written:—'I have no doubt that you would willingly have done this without a fee, but I insist upon your acceptance of the enclosed.' I opened it with some vague notions of an eccentric millionaire and a fifty pound note, but all I found was a postal order for four and sixpence. The whole incident struck me as so whimsical that I laughed until I was tired. You'll find there's so much tragedy in a doctor's life, my boy, that he would not be able to stand it if it were not for the strain of comedy which comes every now and then to leaven it.

"And a doctor has very much to be thankful for also. Don't you ever forget it. It is such a pleasure to do a little good that a man should pay for the privilege instead of being paid for it. Still, of course, he has his home to keep up and his wife and children to support. But his patients are his friends—or they should be so. He goes from house to house, and his step and his voice are loved and welcomed in each. What could a man ask for more than that? And besides, he is forced to be a good man. It is impossible for him to be anything else. How can a man spend his whole life in seeing suffering bravely borne and yet remain a hard or a vicious man? It is a noble, generous, kindly profession, and you youngsters have got to see that it remains so."

XIV

THE DOCTORS OF HOYLAND

Doctor James Ripley was always looked upon as an exceedingly lucky dog by all of the profession who knew him. His father had preceded him in a practice in the village of Hoyland, in the north of Hampshire, and all was ready for him on the very first day that the law allowed him to put his name at the foot of a prescription. In a few years the old gentleman retired, and settled on the South Coast, leaving his son in undisputed possession of the whole country-side. Save for Doctor Horton, near Basingstoke, the young surgeon had a clear run of six miles in every direction, and took his fifteen hundred pounds a year, though, as is usual in country practices, the stable swallowed up most of what the consulting-room earned.

Doctor James Ripley was two-and-thirty years of age, reserved, learned, unmarried, with set, rather stern features, and a thinning of the dark hair upon the top of his head, which was worth quite a hundred a year to him. He was particularly happy in his management of ladies. He had caught the tone of bland sternness and decisive suavity which dominates without offending. Ladies, however, were not equally happy in their management of him. Professionally, he was always at their service. Socially, he was a drop of quicksilver. In vain the country mammas spread out their simple lures in front of him. Dances and picnics were not to his taste, and he preferred during his scanty leisure to shut himself up in his study, and to bury himself in Virchow's Archives and the professional journals.

Study was a passion with him, and he would have none of the rust which often gathers round a country practitioner. It was his ambition to keep his knowledge as fresh and bright as at the moment when he had stepped out of the examination hall. He prided himself on being able at a moment's notice to rattle off the seven ramifications of some obscure artery, or to give the exact percentage of any physiological compound. After a long day's work he would sit up half the night performing iridectomies and extractions upon the sheep's eyes sent in by the village butcher, to the horror of his housekeeper, who had to remove the débris next morning. His love for his work was the one fanaticism which found a place in his dry, precise nature.

It was the more to his credit that he should keep up to date in his knowledge, since he had no competition to force him to exertion. In the seven years during which he had practiced in Hoyland three rivals had pitted themselves against him, two in the village itself and one in the neighbouring hamlet of Lower Hoyland. Of these one had sickened and wasted, being, as it was said, himself the only patient whom he had treated during his eighteen months of ruralising. A second had bought a fourth share of a Basingstoke practice, and had departed honourably, while a third had vanished one September night, leaving a gutted house and an unpaid drug bill behind him. Since then the district had become a monopoly, and no one had dared to measure himself against the established fame of the Hoyland doctor.

It was, then, with a feeling of some surprise and considerable curiosity that on driving through Lower Hoyland one morning he perceived that the new house at the end of the village was occupied, and that a virgin brass plate glistened upon the swinging gate which faced the high road. He pulled up his fifty guinea chestnut mare and took a good look at it. "Verrinder Smith, M.D.," was printed across it in very neat, small lettering. The last man had had letters half a foot long, with a lamp like a fire-station. Doctor James Ripley noted the difference, and deduced from it that the new-comer might possibly prove a more formidable opponent. He was convinced of it that evening when he came to consult the current medical directory. By it he learned that Doctor Verrinder Smith was the holder of superb degrees, that he had studied with distinction at Edinburgh, Paris, Berlin, and Vienna, and finally that he had been awarded a gold medal and the Lee Hopkins scholarship for original research, in recognition of an exhaustive inquiry into the functions of the anterior spinal nerve roots. Doctor Ripley passed his fingers through his thin hair in bewilderment as he read his rival's record. What on earth could so brilliant a man mean by putting up his plate in a little Hampshire hamlet.

But Doctor Ripley furnished himself with an explanation to the riddle. No doubt Dr. Verrinder Smith had simply come down there in order to pursue some scientific research in peace and quiet. The plate was up as an address rather than as an invitation to patients. Of course, that must be the true explanation. In that case the presence of this brilliant neighbour would be a splendid thing for his own studies. He had often longed for some kindred mind, some steel on which he might strike his flint. Chance had brought it to him, and he rejoiced exceedingly.

And this joy it was which led him to take a step which was quite at variance with his usual habits. It is the custom for a new-comer among medical men to call first upon the older, and the etiquette upon the subject is strict. Doctor Ripley was pedantically exact on such points, and yet he deliberately drove over next day and called upon Doctor Verrinder Smith. Such a waiving of ceremony was, he felt, a gracious act upon his part, and a fit prelude to the intimate relations which he hoped to establish with his neighbour.

The house was neat and well appointed, and Doctor Ripley was shown by a smart maid into a dapper little consulting-room. As he passed in he noticed two or three parasols and a lady's sun-bonnet hanging in the hall. It was a pity that his colleague should be a married man. It would put them upon a different footing, and interfere with those long evenings of high scientific talk which he had pictured to himself. On the other hand, there was much in the consulting-room to please him. Elaborate instruments, seen more often in hospitals than in the houses of private practitioners, were scattered about. A sphygmograph stood upon the table and a gasometer-like engine, which was new to Doctor Ripley, in the corner. A bookcase full of ponderous volumes in French and German, paper-covered for the most part, and varying in tint from the shell to the yolk of a duck's egg, caught his wandering eyes, and he was deeply absorbed in their titles when the door opened suddenly behind him. Turning round, he found himself facing a little woman, whose plain, palish face was remarkable only for a pair of shrewd, humorous eyes of a blue which had two shades too much green in it. She held a pince-nez in her left hand, and the doctor's card in her right.

"How do you do, Doctor Ripley?" said she.

"How do you do, madam?" returned the visitor. "Your husband is perhaps out?"

"I am not married," said she simply.

"Oh, I beg your pardon! I meant the doctor—Dr. Verrinder Smith."

"I am Doctor Verrinder Smith."

Doctor Ripley was so surprised that he dropped his hat and forgot to pick it up again.

"What!" he gasped, "the Lee Hopkins prizeman! You!"

He had never seen a woman doctor before, and his whole conservative soul rose up in revolt at the idea. He could not recall any Biblical injunction that the man should remain ever the doctor and the woman the nurse, and yet he felt as if a blasphemy had been committed. His face betrayed his feelings only too clearly.

"I am sorry to disappoint you," said the lady drily.

"You certainly have surprised me," he answered, picking up his hat.

"You are not among our champions, then?"

"I cannot say that the movement has my approval."

"And why?"

"I should much prefer not to discuss it."

"But I am sure you will answer a lady's question."

"Ladies are in danger of losing their privileges when they usurp the place of the other sex. They cannot claim both."

"Why should a woman not earn her bread by her brains?"

Doctor Ripley felt irritated by the quiet manner in which the lady cross-questioned him.

"I should much prefer not to be led into a discussion, Miss Smith."

"Doctor Smith," she interrupted.

"Well, Doctor Smith! But if you insist upon an answer, I must say that I do not think medicine a suitable profession for women and that I have a personal objection to masculine ladies."

It was an exceedingly rude speech, and he was ashamed of it, the instant after he had made it. The lady however, simply raised her eyebrows and smiled.

"It seems to me that you are begging the question," said she. "Of course, if it makes women masculine that would be a considerable deterioration."

It was a neat little counter, and Doctor Ripley, like a pinked fencer, bowed his acknowledgment.

"I must go," said he.

"I am sorry that we cannot come to some more friendly conclusion since we are to be neighbours," she remarked.

He bowed again, and took a step towards the door.

"It was a singular coincidence," she continued, "that at the instant that you called I was reading your paper on 'Locomotor Ataxia,' in the Lancet."

"Indeed," said he drily.

"I thought it was a very able monograph."

"You are very good."

"But the views which you attribute to Professor Pitres, of Bordeaux, have been repudiated by him."

"I have his pamphlet of 1890," said Doctor Ripley angrily.

"Here is his pamphlet of 1891." She picked it from among a litter of periodicals. "If you have time to glance your eye down this passage——"

Doctor Ripley took it from her and shot rapidly through the paragraph which she indicated. There was no denying that it completely knocked the bottom out of his own article. He threw it down, and with another frigid bow he made for the door. As he took the reins from the groom he glanced round and saw that the lady was standing at her window, and it seemed to him that she was laughing heartily.

All day the memory of this interview haunted him. He felt that he had come very badly out of it. She had showed herself to be his superior on his own pet subject. She had been courteous while he had been rude, self-possessed when he had been angry. And then, above all, there was her presence, her monstrous intrusion to rankle in his mind. A woman doctor had been an abstract thing before, repugnant but distant. Now she was there in actual practice, with a brass plate up just like his own, competing for the same patients. Not that he feared competition, but he objected to this lowering of his ideal of womanhood. She could not be more than thirty, and had a bright, mobile face, too. He thought of her humorous eyes, and of her strong, well-turned chin. It revolted him the more to recall the details of her education. A man, of course, could come through such an ordeal with all his purity, but it was nothing short of shameless in a woman.

But it was not long before he learned that even her competition was a thing to be feared. The novelty of her presence had brought a few curious invalids into her consulting-rooms, and, once there, they had been so impressed by the firmness of her manner and by the singular, new-fashioned instruments with which she tapped, and peered, and sounded, that it formed the core of their conversation for weeks afterwards. And soon there were tangible proofs of her powers upon the country-side. Farmer Eyton, whose callous ulcer had been quietly spreading over his shin for years back under a gentle régime of zinc ointment, was painted round with blistering fluid, and found, after three blasphemous nights, that his sore was stimulated into healing. Mrs. Crowder, who had always regarded the birthmark upon her second daughter Eliza as a sign of the indignation of the Creator at a third helping of raspberry tart which she had partaken of during a critical period, learned that, with the help of two galvanic needles, the mischief was not irreparable. In a month Doctor Verrinder Smith was known, and in two she was famous.

Occasionally, Doctor Ripley met her as he drove upon his rounds. She had started a high dog-cart, taking the reins herself, with a little tiger behind. When they met he invariably raised his hat with punctilious politeness, but the grim severity of his face showed how formal was the courtesy. In fact, his dislike was rapidly deepening into absolute detestation. "The unsexed woman," was the description of her which he permitted himself to give to those of his patients who still remained staunch. But, indeed, they were a rapidly-decreasing body, and every day his pride was galled by the news of some fresh defection. The lady had somehow impressed the country-folk with almost superstitious belief in her power, and from far and near they flocked to her consulting-room.

But what galled him most of all was, when she did something which he had pronounced to be impracticable. For all his knowledge he lacked nerve as an operator, and usually sent his worst cases up to London. The lady, however, had no weakness of the sort, and took everything that came in her way. It was agony to him to hear that she was about to straighten little Alec Turner's club-foot, and right at the fringe of the rumour came a note from his mother, the rector's wife, asking him if he would be so good as to act as chloroformist. It would be inhumanity to refuse, as there was no other who could take the place, but it was gall and wormwood to his sensitive nature. Yet, in spite of his vexation, he could not but admire the dexterity with which the thing was done. She handled the little wax-like foot so gently, and held the tiny tenotomy knife as an artist holds his pencil. One straight insertion, one snick of a tendon, and it was all over without a stain upon the white towel which lay beneath. He had never seen anything more masterly, and he had the honesty to say so, though her skill increased his dislike of her. The operation spread her fame still further at his expense, and self-preservation was added to his other grounds for detesting her. And this very detestation it was which brought matters to a curious climax.

One winter's night, just as he was rising from his lonely dinner, a groom came riding down from Squire Faircastle's, the richest man in the district, to say that his daughter had scalded her hand, and that medical help was needed on the instant. The coachman had ridden for the lady doctor, for it mattered nothing to the Squire who came as long as it were speedily. Doctor Ripley rushed from his surgery with the determination that she should not effect an entrance into this stronghold of his if hard driving on his part could prevent it. He did not even wait to light his lamps, but sprang into his gig and flew off as fast as hoof could rattle. He lived rather nearer to the Squire's than she did, and was convinced that he could get there well before her.

And so he would but for that whimsical element of chance, which will for ever muddle up the affairs of this world and dumbfound the prophets. Whether it came from the want of his lights, or from his mind being full of the thoughts of his rival, he allowed too little by half a foot in taking the sharp turn upon the Basingstoke road. The empty trap and the frightened horse clattered away into the darkness, while the Squire's groom crawled out of the ditch into which he had been shot. He struck a match, looked down at his groaning companion, and then, after the fashion of rough, strong men when they see what they have not seen before, he was very sick.

The doctor raised himself a little on his elbow in the glint of the match. He caught a glimpse of something white and sharp bristling through his trouser-leg half-way down the shin.

"Compound!" he groaned. "A three months' job," and fainted.

When he came to himself the groom was gone, for he had scudded off to the Squire's house for help, but a small page was holding a gig-lamp in front of his injured leg, and a woman, with an open case of polished instruments gleaming in the yellow light, was deftly slitting up his trouser with a crooked pair of scissors.

"It's all right, doctor," said she soothingly. "I am so sorry about it. You can have Doctor Horton to-morrow, but I am sure you will allow me to help you to-night. I could hardly believe my eyes when I saw you by the roadside."

"The groom has gone for help," groaned the sufferer.

"When it comes we can move you into the gig. A little more light, John! So! Ah, dear, dear, we shall have laceration unless we reduce this before we move you. Allow me to give you a whiff of chloroform, and I have no doubt that I can secure it sufficiently to——"

Doctor Ripley never heard the end of that sentence. He tried to raise a hand and to murmur something in protest, but a sweet smell was in his nostrils, and a sense of rich peace and lethargy stole over his jangled nerves. Down he sank, through clear, cool water, ever down and down into the green shadows beneath, gently, without effort, while the pleasant chiming of a great belfry rose and fell in his ears. Then he rose again, up and up, and ever up, with a terrible tightness about his temples, until at last he shot out of those green shadows and was in the light once more. Two bright, shining, golden spots gleamed before his dazed eyes. He blinked and blinked before he could give a name to them. They were only the two brass balls at the end posts of his bed, and he was lying in his own little room, with a head like a cannon ball, and a leg like an iron bar. Turning his eyes, he saw the calm face of Doctor Verrinder Smith looking down at him.

"Ah, at last!" said she. "I kept you under all the way home, for I knew how painful the jolting would be. It is in good position now with a strong side splint. I have ordered a morphia draught for you. Shall I tell your groom to ride for Doctor Horton in the morning?"

"I should prefer that you should continue the case," said Doctor Ripley feebly, and then, with a half-hysterical laugh—"You have all the rest of the parish as patients, you know, so you may as well make the thing complete by having me also."

It was not a very gracious speech, but it was a look of pity and not of anger which shone in her eyes as she turned away from his bedside.

Doctor Ripley had a brother, William, who was assistant surgeon at a London hospital, and who was down in Hampshire within a few hours of his hearing of the accident. He raised his brows when he heard the details.

"What! You are pestered with one of those!" he cried.

"I don't know what I should have done without her."

"I've no doubt she's an excellent nurse."

"She knows her work as well as you or I."

"Speak for yourself, James," said the London man with a sniff. "But apart from that, you know that the principle of the thing is all wrong."

"You think there is nothing to be said on the other side?"

"Good heavens! do you?"

"Well, I don't know. It struck me during the night that we may have been a little narrow in our views."

"Nonsense, James. It's all very fine for women to win prizes in the lecture-room, but you know as well as I do that they are no use in an emergency. Now I warrant that this woman was all nerves when she was setting your leg. That reminds me that I had better just take a look at it and see that it is all right."

"I would rather that you did not undo it," said the patient. "I have her assurance that it is all right."

Brother William was deeply shocked.

"Of course, if a woman's assurance is of more value than the opinion of the assistant surgeon of a London hospital, there is nothing more to be said," he remarked.

"I should prefer that you did not touch it," said the patient firmly, and Doctor William went back to London that evening in a huff.

The lady, who had heard of his coming, was much surprised on learning of his departure.

"We had a difference upon a point of professional etiquette," said Doctor James, and it was all the explanation he would vouchsafe.

For two long months Doctor Ripley was brought in contact with his rival every day, and he learned many things which he had not known before. She was a charming companion, as well as a most assiduous doctor. Her short presence during the long, weary day was like a flower in a sand waste. What interested him was precisely what interested her, and she could meet him at every point upon equal terms. And yet under all her learning and her firmness ran a sweet, womanly nature, peeping out in her talk, shining in her greenish eyes, showing itself in a thousand subtle ways which the dullest of men could read. And he, though a bit of a prig and a pedant, was by no means dull, and had honesty enough to confess when he was in the wrong.

"I don't know how to apologise to you," he said in his shame-faced fashion one day, when he had progressed so far as to be able to sit in an arm-chair with his leg upon another one; "I feel that I have been quite in the wrong."

"Why, then?"

"Over this woman question. I used to think that a woman must inevitably lose something of her charm if she took up such studies."

"Oh, you don't think they are necessarily unsexed, then?" she cried, with a mischievous smile.

"Please don't recall my idiotic expression."

"I feel so pleased that I should have helped in changing your views. I think that it is the most sincere compliment that I have ever had paid me."

"At any rate, it is the truth," said he, and was happy all night at the remembrance of the flush of pleasure which made her pale face look quite comely for the instant.

For, indeed, he was already far past the stage when he would acknowledge her as the equal of any other woman. Already he could not disguise from himself that she had become the one woman. Her dainty skill, her gentle touch, her sweet presence, the community of their tastes, had all united to hopelessly upset his previous opinions. It was a dark day for him now when his convalescence allowed her to miss a visit, and darker still that other one which he saw approaching when all occasion for her visits would be at an end. It came round at last, however, and he felt that his whole life's fortune would hang upon the issue of that final interview. He was a direct man by nature, so he laid his hand upon hers as it felt for his pulse, and he asked her if she would be his wife.

"What, and unite the practices?" said she.

He started in pain and anger.

"Surely you do not attribute any such base motive to me!" he cried. "I love you as unselfishly as ever a woman was loved."

"No, I was wrong. It was a foolish speech," said she, moving her chair a little back, and tapping her stethoscope upon her knee. "Forget that I ever said it. I am so sorry to cause you any disappointment, and I appreciate most highly the honour which you do me, but what you ask is quite impossible."

With another woman he might have urged the point, but his instincts told him that it was quite useless with this one. Her tone of voice was conclusive. He said nothing, but leaned back in his chair a stricken man.

"I am so sorry," she said again. "If I had known what was passing in your mind I should have told you earlier that I intend to devote my life entirely to science. There are many women with a capacity for marriage, but few with a taste for biology. I will remain true to my own line, then. I came down here while waiting for an opening in the Paris Physiological Laboratory. I have just heard that there is a vacancy for me there, and so you will be troubled no more by my intrusion upon your practice. I have done you an injustice just as you did me one. I thought you narrow and pedantic, with no good quality. I have learned during your illness to appreciate you better, and the recollection of our friendship will always be a very pleasant one to me."

And so it came about that in a very few weeks there was only one doctor in Hoyland. But folks noticed that the one had aged many years in a few months, that a weary sadness lurked always in the depths of his blue eyes, and that he was less concerned than ever with the eligible young ladies whom chance, or their careful country mammas, placed in his way.

XV

CRABBE'S PRACTICE

I wonder how many men remember Tom Waterhouse Crabbe, student of medicine in this city. He was a man whom it was not easy to forget if you had once come across him. Geniuses are more commonly read about than seen, but one could not speak five minutes with Crabbe without recognising that he had inherited some touch of that subtle, indefinable essence. There was a bold originality in his thought, and a convincing earnestness in his mode of expressing it, which pointed to something higher than mere cleverness. He studied spasmodically and irregularly, yet he was one of the first men—certainly the most independent thinker—of his year. Poor Crabbe—there was something delightfully original even in his mistakes. I can remember how he laboriously explained to his examiner that the Spanish fly grew in Spain. And how he gave five drops of Sabin oil credit for producing that state which it is usually believed to rectify.

Crabbe was not at all the type of man whom we usually associate with the word "genius." He was not pale nor thin, neither was his hair of abnormal growth. On the contrary he was a powerfully built, square-shouldered fellow, full of vitality, with a voice like a bull and a laugh that could be heard across the meadows. A muscular Christian too, and one of the best Rugby forwards in Edinburgh.

I remember my first meeting with Crabbe. It gave me a respect both for his cool reasoning powers and for his courage. It was at one of the Bulgarian Atrocity meetings held in Edinburgh in '78. The hall was densely packed and the ventilation defective, so that I was not sorry to find that owing to my lateness I was unable to get any place, and had to stand in the doorway. Leaning against the wall there I could both enjoy the cool air and hear the invectives which speaker after speaker was hurling at the Conservative ministry. The audience seemed enthusiastically unanimous. A burst of cheering hailed every argument and sarcasm. There was not one dissentient voice. The speaker paused to moisten his lips, and there was a silence over the hall. Then a clear voice rose from the middle of it: "All very fine, but what did Gladstone——" There was a howl of execration and yells of "Turn him out!" But the voice was still audible. "What did Gladstone do in '63?" it demanded. "Turn him out. Show him out of the window! Put him out!" There was a perfect hurricane of threats and abuse. Men sprang upon the benches shaking their sticks and peering over each other's shoulders to get a glimpse of the daring Conservative. "What did Gladstone do in '63?" roared the voice; "I insist upon being answered." There was another howl of execration, a great swaying of the crowd, and an eddy in the middle of it. Then the mass of people parted and a man was borne out kicking and striking, and after a desperate resistance was precipitated down the stairs.

As the meeting became somewhat monotonous after this little divertisement, I went down into the street to cool myself. There was my inquisitive friend leaning up against a lamp-post with his coat torn to shreds and a pipe in his mouth. Recognising him by his cut as being a medical student, I took advantage of the freemasonry which exists between members of that profession.

"Excuse me," I said, "you are a medical, aren't you?"

"Yes," he said; "Thomas Crabbe, a 'Varsity man."

"My name is Barton," I said. "Pardon my curiosity, but would you mind telling me what Gladstone did do in '63?"

"My dear chap," said Crabbe, taking my arm and marching up the street with me, "I haven't the remotest idea in the world. You see, I was confoundedly hot and I wanted a smoke, and there seemed no chance of getting out, for I was jammed up right in the middle of the hall, so I thought I'd just make them carry me out; and I did— not a bad idea, was it? If you have nothing better to do, come up to my digs and have some supper."

"Certainly," said I; and that was the foundation of my friendship with Thomas Crabbe.

Crabbe took his degree a year before I did, and went down to a large port in England with the intention of setting up there. A brilliant career seemed to lie before him, for besides his deep knowledge of medicine, acquired in the most practical school in the world, he had that indescribable manner which gains a patient's confidence at once. It is curious how seldom the two are united.

That charming doctor, my dear madam, who pulled the young Charley through the measles so nicely, and had such a pleasant manner and such a clever face, was a noted duffer at college and the laughing-stock of his year. While poor little Doctor Grinder whom you snubbed so, and who seemed so nervous and didn't know where to put his hands, he won a gold medal for original research and was as good a man as his professors. After all, it is generally the outside case, not the inside works, which is noticed in this world.

Crabbe went down with his young degree, and a still younger wife, to settle in this town, which we will call Brisport. I was acting as assistant to a medical man in Manchester, and heard little from my former friend, save that he had set up in considerable style, and was making a bid for a high-class practice at once. I read one most deep and erudite paper in a medical journal, entitled "Curious Development of a Discopherous Bone in the Stomach of a Duck," which emanated from his pen, but beyond this and some remarks on the embryology of fishes he seemed strangely quiet.

One day to my surprise I received a telegram from Mrs. Crabbe begging me to run down to Brisport and see her husband, as he was far from well. Having obtained leave of absence from my principal, I started by the next train, seriously anxious about my friend. Mrs. Crabbe met me at the station. She told me Tom was getting very much broken down by continued anxiety; the expenses of keeping up his establishment were heavy, and patients were few and far between. He wished my advice and knowledge of practical work to guide him in this crisis.

I certainly found Crabbe altered very much for the worse. He looked gaunt and cadaverous, and much of his old reckless joyousness had left him, though he brightened up wonderfully on seeing an old friend.

After dinner the three of us held a solemn council of war, in which he laid before me all his difficulties. "What in the world am I to do, Barton?" he said. "If I could make myself known it would be all right, but no one seems to look at my door-plate, and the place is overstocked with doctors. I believe they think I am a D.D. I wouldn't mind if these other fellows were good men, but they are not. They are all antiquated old fogies at least half a century behind the day. Now there is old Markham, who lives in that brick house over there and does most of the practice in the town. I'll swear he doesn't know the difference between locomotor ataxia and a hypodermic syringe, but he is known, so they flock into his surgery in a manner which is simply repulsive. And Davidson down the road, he is only an L.S.A. Talked about epispastic paralysis at the Society the other night—confused it with liquor epispasticus, you know. Yet that fellow makes a pound to my shilling."

"Get your name known and write," said I.

"But what on earth am I to write about?" asked Crabbe. "If a man has no cases, how in the world is he to describe them? Help yourself and pass the bottle."

"Couldn't you invent a case just to raise the wind?"

"Not a bad idea," said Crabbe thoughtfully. "By the way, did you see my 'Discopherous Bone in a Duck's Stomach'?"

"Yes; it seemed rather good."

"Good, I believe you! Why, man, it was a domino which the old duck had managed to gorge itself with. It was a perfect godsend. Then I wrote about embryology of fishes because I knew nothing about it and reasoned that ninety-nine men in a hundred would be in the same boat. But as to inventing whole cases, it seems rather daring, does it not?"

"A desperate disease needs desperate remedies," said I. "You remember old Hobson at college. He writes once a year to the British Medical and asks if any correspondent can tell him how much it costs to keep a horse in the country. And then he signs himself in the Medical Register as 'The contributor of several unostentatious queries and remarks to scientific papers!'"

It was quite a treat to hear Crabbe laugh with his old student guffaw. "Well, old man," he said, "we'll talk it over to-morrow. We mustn't be selfish and forget that you are a visitor here. Come along out, and see the beauties (save the mark!) of Brisport." So saying he donned a funereal coat, a pair of spectacles, and a hat with a desponding brim, and we spent the remainder of the evening roaming about and discussing mind and matter.

We had another council of war next day. It was a Sunday, and as we sat in the window, smoking our pipes and watching the crowded street, we brooded over many plans for gaining notoriety.

"I've done Bob Sawyer's dodge," said Tom despondingly. "I never go to church without rushing out in the middle of the sermon, but no one knows who I am, so it is no good. I had a nice slide In front of the door last winter for three weeks, and used to give it a polish up after dusk every night. But there was only one man ever fell on it, and he actually limped right across the road to Markham's surgery. Wasn't that hard lines?"

"Very hard indeed," said I.

"Something might be done with orange peel," continued Tom, "but it looks so awfully bad to have the whole pavement yellow with peel in front of a doctor's house."

"It certainly does," I agreed.

"There was one fellow came in with a cut head one night," said Tom, "and I sewed him up, but he had forgotten his purse. He came back in a week to have the stitches taken out, but without the money. That man is going about to this day, Jack, with half a yard of my catgut in him—and in him it'll stay until I see the coin."

"Couldn't we get up some incident," said I, "which would bring your name really prominently before the public?"

"My dear fellow, that's exactly what I want. If I could get my name into the Brisport Chronicle it would be worth five hundred a year to me. There's a family connection, you know, and people only want to realise that I am here. But how am I to do it unless by brawling in the street or by increasing my family? Now, there was the excitement about the discopherous bone. If Huxley or some of these fellows had taken the matter up it might have been the making of me. But they took it all in with a disgusting complacency as if it was the most usual thing in the world and dominoes were the normal food of ducks. I'll tell you what I'll do," he continued, moodily eyeing his fowls. "I'll puncture the floors of their fourth ventricles and present them to Markham. You know that makes them ravenous, and they'd eat him out of house and home in time. Eh, Jack?"

"Look here, Thomas," said I, "you want your name in the papers—is that it?"

"That's about the state of the case."

"Well, by Jove, you shall have it."

"Eh? Why? How?"

"There's a pretty considerable crowd of people outside, isn't there, Tom?" I continued. "They are coming out of church, aren't they? If there was an accident now it would make some noise."

"I say, you're not going to let rip among them with a shot gun, are you, in order to found a practice for me?"

"No, not exactly. But how would this read in tomorrow's Chronicle?—'Painful occurrence in George Street.—As the congregation were leaving George Street Cathedral after the morning service, they were horrified to see a handsome, fashionably dressed gentleman stagger and fall senseless upon the pavement. He was taken up and carried writhing in terrible convulsions into the surgery of the well-known practitioner Doctor Crabbe, who had been promptly upon the spot. We are happy to state that the fit rapidly passed off, and that, owing to the skilful attention which he received, the gentleman, who is a distinguished visitor in our city, was able to regain his hotel and is now rapidly becoming convalescent.' How would that do, eh?"

"Splendid, Jack—splendid!"

"Well, my boy, I'm your fashionably dressed stranger, and I promise you they won't carry me into Markham's."

"My dear fellow, you are a treasure—you won't mind my bleeding you?"

"Bleeding me, confound you! Yes, I do very much mind."

"Just opening a little vein," pleaded Tom.

"Not a capillary," said I. "Now, look here; I'll throw up the whole business unless you give me your word to behave yourself. I don't draw the line at brandy."

"Very well, brandy be it," grumbled Tom.

"Well, I'm off," said I. "I'll go into the fit against your garden gate."

"All right, old man."

"By the way, what sort of a fit would you like? I could give you either an epileptic or an apoplectic easily, but perhaps you'd like something more ornate—a catalepsy or a trade spasm, maybe—with miner's nystagmus or something of that kind?"

"Wait a bit till I think," said Tom, and he sat puffing at his pipe for five minutes. "Sit down again, Jack," he continued. "I think we could do something better than this. You see, a fit isn't a very deadly thing, and if I did bring you through one there would be no credit in it. If we are going to work this thing, we may as well work it well We can only do it once. It wouldn't do for the same fashionably dressed stranger to be turning up a second time. People would begin to smell a rat."

"So they would," said I; "but hang it, you can't expect me to tumble off the cathedral spire, in order that you may hold an inquest on my remains! I You may command me in anything reasonable, however. What shall it be?"

Tom seemed lost in thought. "Can you swim?" he said presently.

"Fairly well."

"You could keep yourself afloat for five minutes?"

"Yes, I could do that."

"You're not afraid of water?"

"I'm not much afraid of anything."

"Then come out," said Tom, "and we'll go over the ground."

I couldn't get one word out of him as to his intentions, so I trotted along beside him, wondering what in the wide world he was going to do. Our first stoppage was at a small dock which is crossed by a swinging iron bridge. He hailed an amphibious man with top-boots. "Do you keep rowing-boats and let them out?" he asked.

"Yes, sir," said the man.

"Then good day," and to the boatman's profound and audible disgust we set off at once in the other direction.

Our next stoppage was at the Jolly Mariner's Arms. Did they keep beds? Yes, they kept beds. We then proceeded to the chemist's. Did he keep a galvanic battery? Once again the answer was in the affirmative, and with a satisfied smile Tom Crabbe headed for home once more, leaving some very angry people behind him.

That evening over a bowl of punch he revealed his plan—and the council of three revised it, modified it, and ended by adopting it, with the immediate result that I at once changed my quarters to the Brisport Hotel.

I was awakened next day by the sun streaming in at my bedroom window. It was a glorious morning. I sprang out of bed and looked at my watch. It was nearly nine o'clock. "Only an hour," I muttered, "and nearly a mile to walk," and proceeded to dress with all the haste I could. "Well," I soliloquised as I sharpened my razor, "if old Tom Crabbe doesn't get his name in the papers to-day, it isn't my fault. I wonder if any friend would do as much for me!" I finished my toilet, swallowed a cup of coffee and sallied out.

Brisport seemed unusually lively this morning. The streets were crowded with people. I wormed my way down Waterloo Street through the old Square and past Crabbe's house. The cathedral bells were chiming ten o'clock as I reached the above-mentioned little dock with the iron swinging bridge. A man was standing on the bridge leaning over the balustrades. There was no mistaking the heart-broken hat rim and the spectacles of Thomas Waterhouse Crabbe, M.B.

I passed him without sign of recognition, dawdled a little on the quay, and then sauntered down to the boathouse. Our friend of yesterday was standing at the door with a short pipe in his mouth.

"Could I have a boat for an hour?" I asked.

He beamed all over. "One minute, sir," he said, "an' I'll get the sculls. Would you want me to row you, sir?"

"Yes, you'd better," I replied.

He bustled about, and in a short time managed to launch a leaky-looking old tub, into which he stepped, while I squatted down in the sheets.

"Take me round the docks," I said. "I want to have a look at the shipping."

"Aye, aye, sir," said he, and away we went, and paddled about the docks for the best part of an hour. At the end of that time we turned back and pulled up to the little quay from which he had started. It was past eleven now and the place was crowded with people. Half Brisport seemed to have concentrated round the iron bridge. The melancholy hat was still visible.

"Shall I pull in, sir?" asked the boatman.

"Give me the sculls," said I. "I want a bit of exercise—let us change places," and I stood up.

"Take care, sir!" yelled the boatman as I gave a stagger. "Look out!" and he made a frantic grab at me, but too late, for with a melodramatic scream I reeled and fell over into the Brisport duck.

I hardly realised what it was I was going to do until I had done it. It was not a pleasant feeling to have the thick, clammy water closing over one's head. I struck the bottom with my feet, and shot up again to the surface. The air seemed alive with shouts. "Heave a rope!" "Where's a boat-hook!" "Catch him!" "There he is!" The boatman managed to hit me me a smart blow on the head with something, an oar, I fancy, and I went down again, but not before I had got my lungs well filled with air. I came up again and my top-booted friend seized me by the hair of my head as if he would tear my scalp off. "Don't struggle!" he yelled, "and I'll save you yet." But I shook him off, and took another plunge. There was no resisting him next time, however, for he got a boat-hook into my collar, and though I kept my head under water as long as possible I was ignominiously hauled to land.

There I lay on the hard stones of the quay, feeling very much inclined to laugh, but looking, no doubt, very blue and ghastly. "He's gone, poor chap!" said some one. "Send for a doctor." "Run, run to Markham." "Quite dead." "Turn him upside down." "Feel his pulse." "Slap him on the back."

"Stop," said a solemn voice—"stop! Can I be of any assistance? I am a medical man. What has occurred?"

"A man drowned," cried a score of voices. "Stand back, make a ring—room for the doctor!"

"My name is Doctor Crabbe. Dear me, poor young gentleman! Drop his hand," he roared at a man who was making for my pulse. "I tell you in such a state the least pressure or impediment to the arterial circulation might prove fatal."

To save my life I couldn't help giving a very audible inward chuckle at Tom's presence of mind. There was a murmur of surprise among the crowd. Tom solemnly took off his hat. "The death rattle!" he whispered. "The young soul has flown—yet perchance science may yet recall it. Bear him up to the tavern."

A shutter was brought, I was solemnly hoisted on to the top of it, and the melancholy cortège passed along the quay, the corpse being really the most cheerful member of the company.

We got to the Mariner's Arms and I was stripped and laid in the best bed. The news of the accident seemed to have spread, for there was a surging crowd in the street, and the staircase was thronged with people. Tom would only admit about a dozen of the more influential of the townspeople into the room, but issued bulletins out of the window every five minutes to the crowd below.

"Quite dead," I heard him roar. "Respiration has ceased—no pulsation—but we still persevere, it is our duty."

"Shall I bring brandy?" said the landlady.

"Yes, and towels, and a hip bath and a basin—but the brandy first."

This sentiment met with the hearty approbation of the corpse.

"Why, he's drinking it," said the landlady, as she applied the glass to my lips.

"Merely an instance of a reflex automatic action," said Tom. "My good woman, any corpse will drink brandy if you only apply it to the glossopharyngeal tract. Stand aside and we will proceed to try Marshall Hall's method of resuscitation."

The citizens stood round in a solemn ring, while Tom stripped off his coat and, climbing on the bed, proceeded to roll me about in a manner which seemed to dislocate every bone in my body.

"Hang it, man, stop!" I growled, but he only paused to make a dart for the window and yell out "No sign of life," and then fell upon me with greater energy than ever. "We will now try Sylvestre's method," he said, when the perspiration was fairly boiling out of him; and with that he seized me again, and performed a series of evolutions even more excruciating than the first. "It is hopeless!" he said at last, stopping and covering my head reverently with the bed-clothes. "Send for the coroner! He has gone to a better land. Here is my card," he continued to an inspector of police who had arrived. "Doctor Crabbe of George Street. You will see that the matter is accurately reported. Poor young man!" And Tom drew his handkerchief across his eyes and walked towards the door, while a groan of sympathy rose from the crowd outside.

He had his hand upon the handle when a thought seemed to strike him, and he turned back. "There is yet a possible hope," he said, "we have not tried the magical effects of electricity—that subtle power, next of kin to nervous force. Is there a chemist's near?"

"Yes, doctor, there's Mr. McLagan just round the corner."

"Then run! run! A human life trembles in the balance—get his strongest battery, quick!" And away went half the crowd racing down the street and tumbling over each other in the effort to be first at Mr. McLagan's. They came back very red and hot, and one of them bore a shining brown mahogany box in his arms which contained the instrument in question.

"Now, gentlemen," said Tom, "I believe I may say that I am the first practitioner in Great Britain who has applied electricity to this use. In my student days I have seen the learned Rokilansky of Vienna employ it in some such way. I apply the negative pole over the solar plexus, while the positive I place on the inner side of the patella. I have seen it produce surprising effects; it may again in this case."

It certainly did. Whether it was an accident or whether Tom's innate reckless devilry got the better of him I cannot say. He himself always swore that it was an accident, but at any rate he sent the strongest current of a most powerful battery rattling and crashing through my system. I gave one ear-splitting yell and landed with a single bound into the middle of the room. I was charged with electricity like a Leyden jar. My very hair bristled with it.

"You confounded idiot!" I shouted, shaking my fist in Tom's face. "Isn't it enough to dislocate every bone in my body with your ridiculous resuscitations without ruining my constitution with this thing?" and I gave a vicious kick at the mahogany box. Never was there such a stampede! The inspector of police and the correspondent of the Chronicle sprang down the staircase, followed by the twelve respectable citizens. The landlady crawled under the bed. A lodger who was nursing her baby while she conversed with a neighbour in the street below let the child drop upon her friend's head. In fact Tom might have founded the nucleus of a practice there and then. As it was, his usual presence of mind carried him through. "A miracle!" he yelled from the window. "A miracle! Our friend has been brought back to us; send for a cab." And then sotto voce, "For goodness' sake, Jack, behave like a Christian and crawl into bed again. Remember the landlady is in the room and don't go prancing about in your shirt."

"Hang the landlady," said I, "I feel like a lightning conductor—you've ruined me!"

"Poor fellow," cried Tom, once more addressing the crowd, "he is alive, but his intellect is irretrievably affected. He thinks he is a lightning conductor. Make way for the cab. That's right! Now help me to lead him in. He is out of all danger now. He can dress at his hotel. If any of you have any information to give which may throw light upon this case my address is 81 George Street. Remember, Doctor Crabbe, 81 George Street. Good day, kind friends, good-bye!" And with that he bundled me into the cab to prevent my making any further disclosures, and drove off amid the enthusiastic cheers of the admiring crowd.

I could not stay in Brisport long enough to see the effect of my coup d'état. Tom gave us a champagne supper that night, and the fun was fast and furious, but in the midst of it a telegram from my principal was handed in ordering me to return to Manchester by the next train. I waited long enough to get an early copy of the Brisport Chronicle, and beguiled the tedious journey by perusing the glowing account of my mishap. A column and a half was devoted to Dr. Crabbe and the extraordinary effects of electricity upon a drowned man. It ultimately got into some of the London papers, and was gravely commented upon in the Lancet.

As to the pecuniary success of our little experiment I can only judge from the following letter from Tom Crabbe, which I transcribe exactly as I received it:

"What Ho! My resuscitated Corpse,

"You want to know how all goes in Brisport, I suppose. Well, I'll tell you. I'm cutting Markham and Davidson out completely, my boy. The day after our little joke I got a bruised leg (that baby), a cut head (the woman the baby fell upon), an erysipelas, and a bronchitis. Next day a fine rich cancer of Markham's threw him up and came over to me. Also a pneumonia and a man who swallowed a sixpence. I've never had a day since without half a dozen new names on the list, and I'm going to start a trap this week. Just let me know when you are going to set up, and I'll manage to run down, old man, and give you a start in business, if I have to stand on my head in the water-butt. Good-bye. Love from the Missus.

"Ever yours,

"Thomas Waterhouse Crabbe,

"M.B. Edin.

"81 George Street,

"Brisport."

End of the book.

Printed in Great Britain
by Amazon.co.uk, Ltd.,
Marston Gate.